ESSENTIAL MESSAGES FROM GOD'S SERVANTS

masterWork

Lessons from
ANGELS
by Billy Graham

LIVING ON THE RAGGED EDGE
by Charles Swindoll

WINTER 2004-05

LifeWay
CHURCH RESOURCES
Biblical Solutions for Life

Ross H. McLaren
Editor in Chief

Gena Rogers
Editor

René A. Holt
Copy Editor

Brent Bruce
Graphic Design Specialist

Melissa Finn
Lead Technical Specialist

John McClendon
Mic Morrow
Adult Ministry Specialists

Send questions/comments to
   Editor, *MasterWork*
   One LifeWay Plaza
   Nashville, TN 37234-0175
   Or make comments on the web at
   www.lifeway.com

Management Personnel

Louis B. Hanks, *Director*
Publishing

Gary Hauk, *Director*
Leadership and Adult Publishing

Ron Brown, Bill Craig
Managing Directors
Leadership and Adult Publishing

Alan Raughton, *Director*
Church Strategies

ACKNOWLEDGMENTS.–We believe the Bible has God for its author; salvation for its end; and truth, without any mixture of error, for its matter and that all Scripture is totally true and trustworthy. The 2000 statement of *The Baptist Faith and Message* is our doctrinal guideline.

Unless otherwise indicated, all Scripture quotations in the lessons from *Angels* are from the *King James Version*. This translation is available in a Holman Bible and can be ordered through LifeWay Christian Stores. Unless otherwise indicated, all Scripture quotations in the lessons from *Living on the Ragged Edge* are from the *New American Standard Bible*. © The Lockman Foundation, 1960, 1962, 1963, 1968, 1971, 1972, 1973, 1975, 1977. Quotations in the "How to Become a Christian" article or those marked HCSB are taken from the *Holman Christian Standard Bible®*, copyright © 1999, 2000, 2002, 2003 by Holman Bible Publishers. Used by permission. This translation is available in a Holman Bible and can be ordered through LifeWay Christian Stores. Quotations marked AB are from *The Amplified Bible, Old Testament*. Copyright © 1962, 1964 by Zondervan Publishing House. Used by permission. Quotations from *The Amplified New Testament* © The Lockman Foundation 1954, 1958, 1987. Used by permission. Verses marked *Living Bible* are taken from *The Living Bible*. Copyright © Tyndale House Publishers, Wheaton, Illinois, 1971. Used by permission. Passages marked NASB are from the *New American Standard Bible*. © The Lockman Foundation, 1960, 1962, 1963, 1968, 1971, 1972, 1973, 1975, 1977. Used by permission. This translation is available in a Holman Bible and can be ordered through Lifeway Christian Stores. Quotations marked NIV are from the Holy Bible, *New International Version*, copyright © 1973, 1978, 1984 by International Bible Society. This translation is available in a Holman Bible and can be ordered through Lifeway Christian Stores. Quotations marked RSV are from the *Revised Standard Version of the Bible*, copyright 1946, 1952, © 1971, 1973 by the Division of Christian Education of the National Council of Churches of Christ in the U.S.A., and used by permission. Quotations marked TEV are from the *Good News Bible*, the Bible in Today's Modern English Version. Old Testament: Copyright © American Bible Society 1976; New Testament: Copyright © American Bible Society 1966, 1971, 1976. Used by permission.

MasterWork: Essential Messages from God's Servants (ISSN 1542-703X) is published quarterly by LifeWay Christian Resources of the Southern Baptist Convention, One LifeWay Plaza, Nashville, Tennessee 37234; James T. Draper, Jr., President, and Ted Warren, Executive Vice-President. © Copyright 2004 LifeWay Christian Resources of the Southern Baptist Convention. All rights reserved. Single subscription to individual address, $26.35 per year. If you need help with an order, WRITE LifeWay Church Resources Customer Service, One LifeWay Plaza, Nashville, Tennessee 37234-0113; For subscriptions, FAX (615) 251-5818 or EMAIL *subscribe@lifeway.com*. For bulk shipments mailed quarterly to one address, FAX (615) 251-5933 or EMAIL *CustomerService@lifeway.com*. Order ONLINE at *www.lifeway.com*. Mail address changes to: *MasterWork*, One LifeWay Plaza, Nashville, TN 37234-0113.

Printed in the United States of America.

Cover image: © Robert Holmes/CORBIS

table of contents

HOW TO BECOME A CHRISTIAN — 2

Book One

ABOUT THE WRITER *Billy Graham* — 4

INTRODUCING *Angels* — 5

Week of **December 5** — Angels Are for Real — 6

Week of **December 12** — Angelic Organization, Watchfulness, and Roles in Judgment — 18

Week of **December 19** — Angels, the Good News, and the Birth of Jesus — 30

Week of **December 26** — Angels: Now and in the Future — 42

Book Two

ABOUT THE WRITER *Charles Swindoll* — 54

INTRODUCING *Living on the Ragged Edge* — 55

Week of **January 2** — Chasing the Wind — 56

Week of **January 9** — More Miles of Bad Road — 68

Week of **January 16** — Interlude of Rare Insight — 81

Week of **January 23** — One Plus One Equals Survival — 94

Week of **January 30** — A Change in Scenery — 107

Week of **February 6** — Benefits of Wisdom — 119

Week of **February 13** — Mysteries that Defy Explanation — 131

Week of **February 20** — An Objective View of the Rat Race — 143

Week of **February 27** — What Are You Waiting For? — 156

ABOUT THE WRITERS

Billy Graham

wrote the lessons in the Study Theme on angels.

Dr. Graham is a world-renowned evangelist, preacher, and author. He is the founder of the *Billy Graham Evangelistic Association* in Minneapolis, Minnesota. He and his wife Ruth live in Montreat, North Carolina.

AMY SUMMERS wrote the personal learning activities and teaching plans this quarter. Amy is an experienced writer for LifeWay Bible study curriculum, a wife, a mother, and a Sunday School leader from Arden, North Carolina. She is a graduate of Baylor University and Southwestern Baptist Theological Seminary

masterWork:
Essential Messages from God's Servants

• Designed for developing and maturing believers who desire to go deeper into the spiritual truths of God's Word.

• Ideal for many types of Bible study groups.

• A continuing series from leading Christian authors and their key messages.

• Based on LifeWay's well-known, interactive model for daily Bible study.

• The interspersed interactive personal learning activities **in bold type** are written by the writer identified on the Study Theme unit page.

• Teaching plans follow each lesson to help facilitators guide learners through lessons.

• Published quarterly.

ABOUT THIS STUDY

Circle the word that best describes your attitude as you approach this study about angels.

Skeptical   **Curious**   **Eager**   **Indifferent**

In the space below, outline what you already know about angels.

_____

_____

_____

_____

Angels

Why have a series of Bible studies on angels? Isn't talking about angels merely adding to the speculation about supernatural phenomena? What possible value is there in such a discussion? Didn't the fascination with angels vanish with the Middle Ages?

I am convinced that these heavenly beings exist and that they provide unseen aid on our behalf. I do not believe in angels because someone has told me about a dramatic visitation from an angel, impressive as such rare testimonies may be. I do not believe in angels because I have ever seen one—because I haven't. I believe in angels because the Bible says there are angels; and I believe the Bible to be the true Word of God. I also believe in angels because I have sensed their presence in my life on special occasions.

So what I have to say in the lessons that follow will not be an accumulation of my ideas about the spirit world, nor even a reflection of my own spiritual experiences in the spirit realm. I propose to put forward, at least in part, what I understand the Bible to say about angels. Naturally, this will not be an exhaustive study of the subject. I hope, however, that it will arouse your curiosity sufficiently for you to dig out from the Bible all that you can find on this subject after you have studied these lessons. More than that, it is my prayer that you will discover the reality of God's love and care for you as evidenced in the ministry of His angels on your behalf, and that you would go forth in faith each day trusting God's constant watch-care over you.

Billy Graham

Billy GRAHAM

Angels Are for Real

day One

"Angels are among the invisible things made by God."—Billy Graham

Angels Are Created Beings

Don't believe everything you hear or read about angels! Some people would have us believe that angels are only spiritual will-o'-the-wisps. Others view them as celestial beings with beautiful wings and bowed heads.

Describe what picture comes to your mind when you hear the word *angel*. (If you are artistically inclined, sketch your impression of angels in the margin.)

The Bible states that angels, like human beings, were created by God. At one time no angels existed. The apostle Paul wrote, "For by him were all things created, that are in heaven, and that are in earth, visible and invisible." Angels indeed are among the invisible things made by God, for "all things were created by him, and for him" (Colossians 1:16).

The empire of angels is as vast as God's creation. Some biblical scholars believe that angels can be numbered potentially in the millions since Hebrews 12:22 speaks of "an innumerable company of angels." This verse literally says "myriads of angels"—a great but indefinite number. As to their number, David recorded twenty thousand coursing through the skyways of the stars. Even with his limited vision he impressively notes, "The chariots of God are twenty thousand, even thousands of angels" (Psalm 68:17).

Week of DECEMBER 5

Ten thousand angels came down on Mount Sinai to confirm the holy presence of God as He gave the Law to Moses (Deuteronomy 33:2). An earthquake shook the mountain. Moses was held in speech-bound wonder at this mighty cataclysm attended by the visitation of heavenly beings.

Read Revelation 5:11-12. How many angels did John see in his vision? (circle)
A few
Several thousand
A couple of hundred
Too many to count

What were the angels doing? _____
_____

The Book of Revelation also says that armies of angels will appear with Jesus at the Battle of Armageddon when God's foes gather for their final defeat.

Think of it! Multitudes of angels, indescribably mighty, performing the commands of heaven! More amazingly, even one angel is indescribably mighty, as though an extension of the arm of God. Singly or corporately, angels are for real. They are better organized than were the armies of Alexander the Great, Napoleon, or Eisenhower.

Indicate on the line below how convinced you are that angels are real, numerous, and powerfully organized.

|—————|—————|—————|—————|
Not convinced   Totally convinced

day Two

Angels Are Not to Be Worshiped

It is no mere accident that angels are usually invisible. Though God in His infinite wisdom does not, as a rule, permit angels to take on physical dimensions, people tend to venerate them in a fashion that borders on worship. We are warned against worshiping the creature rather than the

> "I am the Lord thy God, which have brought thee out of the land of Egypt, out of the house of bondage. Thou shalt have no other gods before me"
> (Ex. 20:2-3, KJV).

Creator (Romans 1:24-25). It's no less than heretical, and indeed is a breach of the first commandment, to worship any manifestation of angelic presence, patron or blesser.

Paul pointed out that while unusual manifestations may be deeply significant, Jesus Christ the incarnate God, the second person of the Trinity, who is creator of all things and by whom all things exist, is worthy of our worship (Colossians 2:18). We are not to pray to angels. Nor are we to engage in "a voluntary humility and worshiping" of them. Only the Triune God is to be the object of our worship and of our prayers.

Moreover, we should not confuse angels, whether visible or invisible, with the Holy Spirit, the third person of the Trinity and Himself God. Angels do not indwell people; the Holy Spirit seals believers and indwells them when He has regenerated them. The Holy Spirit is all-knowing, all-present, and all-powerful. Angels are mightier than people, but they are not gods, and they do not possess the attributes of deity.

Read John 16:7-8 and Hebrews 1:14. Underline those listed below who are responsible for convicting people of sin. Circle those who are sent to serve and minister to believers.

Holy Spirit   Church Staff   Angels   Church Members

So far as I know, no Scripture says that the Holy Spirit ever manifested Himself in human form to human beings. Jesus did this in the incarnation. The glorious Holy Spirit can be everywhere at the same time, but no angel can be in more than one place at any given moment.

Both angels and the Holy Spirit are at work in our world to accomplish God's perfect will. Frankly, we may not always know the agent or means God is using—the Holy Spirit or the angels—when we discern God's hand at work. We can be sure, however, that there is no contradiction or competition between God the Holy Spirit and God's command of the angelic hosts. God Himself is in control to accomplish His will—and in that we can rejoice!

God uses angels to work out the destinies of men and nations. He has altered the courses of the busy political and social arenas of our society and directed people's destinies by angelic visitation many times over. We must be aware that angels keep in close and vital contact with all that

Week of DECEMBER 5

is happening on the earth. Their knowledge of earthly matters exceeds that of human beings. We must attest to the invisible presence and unceasing labors of angels. Let us believe that they are here among us. They may not laugh or cry with us, but we do know they delight with us over every victory in our evangelistic endeavors.

Read Luke 15:8-10. If you are a believer, describe what you think happened among the angels when you gave your life to Christ.

_____

_____

Have You Ever Seen an Angel?

In Daniel 6:22 we read, "My God hath sent his angel, and hath shut the lions' mouths." In the lion's den, Daniel's sight evidently perceived the angelic presence, and the lions' strength more than met its match in the power of the angel. In most instances, angels, when appearing visibly, are so glorious and impressively beautiful as to stun and amaze those who witness their presence.

Read Matthew 28:1-4. Describe:

1. the actions of the angel at Jesus' empty tomb.

_____

2. the appearance of the angel.

_____

3. the response of others to the angel.

_____

"I looked up, and there was a man dressed in linen ... His body was like topaz, his face like the brilliance of lightning, his eyes like flaming torches, his arms and feet like the gleam of polished bronze, and the sound of his words like the sound of a multitude" (Dan. 10:5-6, HCSB).

"Then I saw another mighty angel coming down from heaven, surrounded by a cloud, with a rainbow over his head. His face was like the sun, his legs were like fiery pillars" (Rev. 10:1, HCSB).

Incidentally, that stone weighed several times more than a single man could move, yet the physical power of the angel was not taxed in rolling it aside.

Abraham, Lot, Jacob, and others had no difficulty recognizing angels when God allowed them to manifest themselves in physical form. Notice, for example, Jacob's instant recognition of angels in Genesis 32:1,2: "And Jacob went on his way, and the angels of God met him. And when Jacob saw them, he said, This is God's host: and he called the name of that place Mahanaim."

Further, both Daniel and John described the glories of the angels (Daniel 10:6 and Revelation 10:1) visibly descending from heaven with immeasurable beauty and brilliance, shining like the sun. Who has not thrilled to read the account of the three Hebrew children, Shadrach, Meshach, and Abednego? They refused to fall in line with the music of obeisance and worship the king of Babylon. They learned that the angel presence can be observed on occasion by people in the unbelieving world on the outside. After they had refused to bow, the angel preserved them from being burned alive or even having the smell of smoke on their garments from the seven-times-hotter fire. The angel came to them in the midst of the flame without harm and was seen by the king, who said, "I see four men . . . in the midst of the fire" (Daniel 3:25).

On the other hand, the Bible indicates angels are more often invisible to human eyes. Whether visible or invisible, however, God causes His angels to go before us, to be with us, and to follow after us.

Yes, angels are real. They are not the product of our imagination but were made by God Himself. Think of it! Whether we see them or not, God has created a vast host of angels to help accomplish His work in this world. When we know God personally through faith in His Son, Jesus Christ, we can have confidence that the angels of God will watch over us and assist us because we belong to Him.

Briefly describe a time you experienced the visible or invisible presence of an angel.

_____

_____

_____

Week of **DECEMBER 5**

How Angels Differ from Humans

The Bible tells us that God has made man "a little lower than the angels." Yet it also says angels are "ministering spirits, sent forth to minister for them who shall be heirs of salvation" (Hebrews 2:5-7; 1:13-14). This sounds like a contradiction: man lower—but eventually higher through redemption. How can we explain this?

First we must remember that this Scripture is speaking both of Jesus Christ and human beings. Jesus did "stoop" when He became man. And as a man He was a little lower than the angels in His humanity—although without losing in any sense His divine nature. But it also speaks about men other than Jesus. God has made human beings head over all the creatures of our earthly world, but they are lower than angels with respect to their bodies and to their place while here on earth.

God commands angels to help humans since they will be made higher than the angels at the resurrection. So says Jesus in Luke 20:36. God will alter the temporary lower position of human beings when the kingdom of God has come in its fullness.

Now let us examine in detail how God says angels differ from humans. Although angels are glorious beings, the Scriptures make it clear that they differ from regenerated human beings in significant ways. How can the angels who have never sinned fully understand what it means to be delivered from sin? How can they understand how precious Jesus is to those for whom His death on Calvary brings light, life, and immortality?

Read 1 Corinthians 6:3. What curious statement about angels did Paul make? _____

Is it not stranger still that angels themselves will be judged by believers who were once sinners? Such judgment, however, apparently applies only to those fallen angels who followed Lucifer.

But even the holy angels have limitations, though the Bible speaks of them as superior to humans in many ways.

11

> "The Spirit Himself testifies together with our spirit that we are God's children, and if children, also heirs— heirs of God and co-heirs with Christ— seeing that we suffer with Him so that we may also be glorified with Him"
> (Rom. 8:16-17, HCSB).

Angels Are Not Heirs of God

Christians are joint heirs with Jesus Christ through redemption (Romans 8:17), which is made theirs by faith in Jesus based on His death at Calvary. Angels who are not joint heirs must stand aside when the believers are introduced to their boundless, eternal riches. The holy angels, however, who are ministering spirits, have never lost their original glory and spiritual relationship with God. This assures them of their exalted place in the royal order of God's creation. By contrast, Jesus identified Himself with fallen human beings in the incarnation when He was "made a little lower than the angels for the suffering of death" (Hebrews 2:9). That He chose to taste the death we deserve also shows that the holy angels do not share our sinfulness—nor our need of redemption.

Angels Cannot Testify of Salvation by Grace Through Faith

Who can comprehend the overwhelming thrill of fellowship with God and the joy of salvation that even angels do not know? When the local church assembles as a group of Christian believers, it represents in the human sphere the highest order of the love of God. No love could go deeper, rise higher, or extend farther than the amazing love that moved God to give His only begotten Son. The angels are aware of that joy (Luke 15:10), and when a person accepts God's gift of eternal life through Jesus Christ angels set all the bells of heaven ringing with their rejoicing before the Lamb of God.

> "And I pray that you, being rooted and established in love, may have power, together with all the saints, to grasp how wide and long and high and deep is the love of Christ"
> (Eph. 3:17-18, NIV).

Yet although the angels rejoice when people are saved and glorify God who has saved them, they cannot do one thing: testify personally to something they have not experienced. They can only point to the experiences of the redeemed and rejoice that God has saved them. This means that throughout eternity we humans alone will give our personal witness to the salvation that God achieved by grace and that we received through faith in Jesus Christ. The person who has never married cannot fully appreciate the wonders of that relationship. The person who has never lost a father or mother cannot understand what the loss means. So angels, great as they are, cannot testify to salvation the same way as those who have experienced it.

Week of DECEMBER 5

What would you tell an angel about what it means to you to be saved by God's grace? Record your comments in the margin.

Angels Have No Experiential Knowledge of the Indwelling God

Nothing in the Bible indicates that the Holy Spirit indwells angels as He does redeemed people. Since He seals believers when they accept Christ, such sealing would be unnecessary for the angels who never fell and who therefore need no salvation.

But there is a second reason for this difference. Redeemed persons on earth have not yet been glorified. Once God has declared them just and given them life, He embarks on a process of making them inwardly holy while they live here below. At death, He makes them perfect. So the Holy Spirit takes His abode in the hearts of all believers while they are still on earth to perform His unique ministry, one that angels cannot perform. God the Father sent Jesus the Son to die. Jesus performed His unique ministry as His part of God's saving process. Likewise, the Holy Spirit has a role, one different from the Son's. Sent by the Father and the Son, the Holy Spirit not only guides and directs believers but also performs a work of grace in their hearts, conforming them to the image of God to make them holy like Christ. Angels cannot provide this sanctifying power.

Furthermore, angels themselves do not need the ministry of the Holy Spirit the way believers do. The angels already have been endowed with authority by virtue of their relationship to God through creation and continuing obedience. They are unspoiled by sin. People, however, are not yet perfect and therefore need what the Holy Spirit alone can give. Someday we will be as perfect as angels are now.

Angels Do Not Marry or Procreate

Read Matthew 22:30. What additional truth about the difference between humans and angels did Jesus point out? _____

Because of this we can make a deduction: The number of angels remains constant. For the obedient angels do not die. The fallen angels

---

If you desire to dig deeper ...

Read the following verses. What additional truths do you learn about the seal of the Holy Spirit?

2 Corinthians 1:21-22:
_____

Ephesians 1:13-14:
_____

will suffer the final judgment at the time God finishes dealing with them. While we cannot be certain, some scholars estimate that as many as one-third of the angels cast their lot with Satan when he mysteriously rebelled against his Creator. In any event, the Book of Hebrews says the angels constitute an "innumerable company," vast hosts that stagger our imagination. A third of them would likely be counted in the hundreds of thousands—ones who are now desperate demons.

Just as angels differ from people with respect to marriage, so they differ in other important ways. Nothing in Scripture says that angels must eat to stay alive. But the Bible says that on certain occasions angels in human form did eat. David refers to the manna eaten by the children of Israel in the wilderness as the bread of angels. In Psalm 78:25, Asaph says, "Man did eat angels' food."

When Abraham was encamped in the plains of Mamre, three angels visited him, of whom one may have been the Lord Jesus (Genesis 18:1-2). These heavenly beings ate and drank what he provided for them by way of customary entertainment. Shortly thereafter, when God decided to destroy Sodom and Gomorrah, two angelic beings came to save backslidden Lot and his family. Lot made them a feast and there again they ate food, including unleavened bread (Genesis 19).

day Five

Angels' Knowledge and Power

Angels excel humankind in their knowledge. When King David was being urged to bring Absalom back to Jerusalem, Joab asked a woman of Teloah to talk to the king. She said: "My lord is wise, according to the wisdom of an angel of God, to know all things that are in the earth" (2 Samuel 14:20). And angels possess knowledge that we humans do not have. But however vast is their knowledge, we can be sure they are not omniscient. They do not know everything. They are not like God.

Week of DECEMBER 5

Read Mark 13:32. Whose knowledge about Jesus' second coming is limited? Check all that apply.

❑ Believers
❑ Angels
❑ The Son in human form
❑ God the Father

Angels probably know things about us that we do not know about ourselves. And because they are ministering spirits, they will always use this knowledge for our good and not for evil purposes. In a day when few people can be trusted with secret information, it is comforting to know that angels will not divulge their great knowledge to hurt us. Rather, they will use it for our good.

Angels enjoy far greater power than humans, but they are not omnipotent or "all powerful." In 2 Thessalonians 1:7, Paul refers to the "mighty angels of God." From the word translated "mighty" here we get the English word *dynamite*. In material power, angels are God's dynamite! In 1 Peter we read, "angels who are greater in might and power [than men] do not bring a reviling judgment against them before the Lord" (2 Peter 2:11, NASB). Peter's testimony here reinforces Paul's.

In Psalm 103:20 David speaks about [God's] "angels that excel in strength." Nowhere in Scripture is that strength manifested more dramatically than in the climax of this age. Following the Battle of Armageddon, Scripture pictures what will happen to Satan: He is to be bound and cast into a bottomless pit. But what power, apart from God Himself, can do this to Satan, whose power we all know about and whose evil designs we have experienced?

Read Daniel 6:22 and Revelation 20:1-3. Circle the number of angels it took to deliver Daniel from the lions. Underline the number of angels necessary to bind Satan and throw him into the pit.

❑ Ten thousand upon ten thousand
❑ Six hundred upon six hundred
❑ One

How great is the power of one of God's mighty angels!

NOTES

To the Leader:

In these teaching plans you will be given two options to create interest at the beginning of the session. The first option is geared more toward a discussion format. The second option may be a little more creative or interactive. Adapt one or both options until you have a create-interest step that will best foster an atmosphere of transformational learning for your class.

Before the Session

1. Prayerfully choose the teaching steps that will help your class explore the material in this week's lesson.
2. Create a display of popular depictions of angels. (You can use Christmas decorations and cards or pictures of angels from TV or movie specials.)
3. Provide a sheet of paper for each participant.
4. Obtain a camera flash or video camera with a bright light.
5. Print Hebrews 1:14 on a large poster. Display this poster throughout the entire unit of study.

During the Session

1. Draw attention to the angel display. Invite volunteers to state the first word that comes to mind when they hear the word *angel*. Ask: *Where do most people get their concept of angels? Are those reliable sources? Why?* Comment that for this week and the next three weeks you will explore the truth about angels. OR Give a sheet of paper to each participant. Ask adults to get in groups of threes and list all the different places they have seen images of angels in the past week. (Consider playing a song about angels during this activity.) After several moments, invite volunteers to relate the most common places images of angels were spotted this week. Ask how many participants saw a REAL angel this week. State that this four-week study may challenge them to understand angels in new ways.
2. Invite someone to read Colossians 1:16. Request a volunteer read the quotation in the margin of Day 1. Discuss how that truth should lead learners to view angels differently from popular notions of angels. Invite volunteers to read aloud Deuteronomy 33:2; Psalm 68:17; Hebrews 12:22; and Revelation 5:11-12. Request participants explore truths about angels that are common to all four passages. (Responses may include the vast number of angels and that angels accompany, worship, and serve God).

Week of DECEMBER 5

3. Ask: *Since angels are heavenly beings, is it OK to worship or to pray to angels? Why?* Ask why some people in today's society tend to worship angels. Use the material and activities in Day 2 to explore the difference between angels and God's Holy Spirit.

4. Ask someone to read aloud the title for Day 3. Point to the angel display and comment that if the only angels that participants have seen resemble the angels on display then they would have to answer no to that question. Turn off the light in the room and either flash a camera flash several times or turn on a video camera light. Ask participants what they see. Comment that if they were ever to see an angel it would be more like a blinding light than the popular depiction of a gentle winged woman. Discuss the first activity of Day 3. Request someone read Daniel 10:5-6 in the margin of Day 3. Ask: *Was Daniel speaking like a teenager, putting "like" in front of every statement or is there another reason for him stating the angel was "like topaz" and "like lightning"?* Explain that Daniel was trying to use earthly words to describe a heavenly creature. Read Daniel 10:7-9 and ask how the response to the angel in this passage is similar to the response in Matthew 28. Read Daniel 10:10-11 and ask: *Why do you think the angel told Daniel to stand? What was the angel's purpose for coming to Daniel? Who sent the angel?* Invite participants to share their responses to the final activity of Day 3. Draw attention to the poster you made of Hebrews 1:14 and lead the class to read the verse aloud in unison. Remind learners the glory must go to God when an angel ministers to them because God sent that angel.

5. Ask: *How are cats different from dogs? Would you rather be a dog or cat? Why? Would you rather be a human or angel? Why? How are angels different from humans?* Use the material, Scriptures in the margin, and activities in Day 4 to explore the last question.

6. Ask how angels' knowledge and power compare to that of human beings. (Use the material in Day 5 to facilitate the discussion.) Request a volunteer read 1 Peter 2:11. Ask: *What can we learn from angels about controlling the power we have?*

7. Ask how angels' knowledge and power compare to that of God. Remind participants that no matter how powerful and fascinating angels are, a believer's focus must always be on worshiping and serving God. Read Psalm 8 as your closing prayer.

NOTES

Billy GRAHAM

Angelic Organization, Watchfulness, and Roles in Judgment

Archangel

"For by him were all things created, that are in heaven, and that are in earth, visible and invisible, whether they be thrones, or dominions, or principalities, or powers: all things were created by him, and for him"
(Col. 1:16, KJV).

We cannot study the subject of angels in the Bible without becoming aware of ranks among angelic beings. The evidence shows that they are organized in terms of authority and glory.

Though some see the ranking of celestial powers as conjectural, it seems to follow this pattern: archangels, angels, seraphim, cherubim, principalities, authorities, powers, thrones, might and dominion (Colossians 1:16; Romans 8:38).

Medieval theologians divided angelic beings into ten grades. Some people, however, have asked whether some of these grades—the principalities, authorities, powers, thrones, might and dominion—could not refer to human institutions and human beings. To answer, we must understand Colossians 1:16. Paul is speaking about creation of things both seen and unseen. Perhaps any list that ranks angelic beings will err, but we can be sure they differ in power, some having authority others do not possess. While I do not wish to be dogmatic, I think there are different ranks of angels and that the list given in Colossians does refer to these celestial personalities. Let's look at just four of them.

Read Jude 9. Who is identified as the archangel?

Gabriel   **Monica**   **Michael**   **Clarence**

We have biblical grounds for believing that before his fall Lucifer was also an archangel, equal or perhaps superior to Michael. The prefix "arch"

Week of DECEMBER 12

suggests a chief, principal, or great angel. Thus, Michael is now the angel above all angels, recognized in rank to be the first prince of heaven. He is, as it were, the Prime Minister in God's administration of the universe and is the "angel administrator" of God for judgment. He must stand alone, because the Bible never speaks of archangels, only the archangel. His name means "who is like unto the Lord."

If you desire to dig deeper ...

Read about the fall of Satan in Isaiah 14:12-15.

Read Daniel 12:1. What special role did Michael perform for the nation of Israel? _____

Do you think that ancient role has any significance to your own life? ❏ Yes ❏ No ❏ Not sure
If so, what? _____

In the Old Testament, Michael seems to be identified primarily with Israel as a nation. Thus, God speaks of Michael as prince of His chosen people (Daniel 12:1). Michael especially protects and defends God's people whoever they are.

Further, in the Book of Daniel Michael is referred to as "Michael, your prince" (Daniel 10:21). He is God's messenger of law and judgment. In this capacity he appears in Revelation 12:7-12 leading the armies that battle Satan, the great dragon, and all of his demons. Michael, with his angels, will be locked in the titanic struggle of the universe at the last conflict of the age, which will mark the defeat of Satan and all forces of darkness. Scripture tells us in advance that Michael will finally be victorious in the battle. Hell will tremble; heaven will rejoice and celebrate!

Read 1 Thessalonians 4:16. What additional privilege and responsibility will Michael have?

_____

Michael, the archangel, will shout as he accompanies Jesus at His Second Coming. Not only does he proclaim the matchless and exciting news that Jesus Christ returns, but he speaks the word of life to all who are dead in Christ and who await their resurrection.

day Two

The Angel Gabriel

Gabriel is one of the most prominent angels mentioned in Scripture. *Gabriel,* in Hebrew, means "God's hero," or "the mighty one," or "God is great." Scripture frequently refers to him as "the messenger of Jehovah" or "the Lord's messenger." However, contrary to popular opinion and to the poet John Milton, Scripture never calls Gabriel an archangel. Yet it refers to his work more often than to Michael's.

Ministry of Gabriel

Read in the margin the four instances Gabriel is mentioned in the Bible. Circle the word(s) that best describes the type of message Gabriel delivered.

Warning   **Understanding**   **Doom**   **Good News**

Gabriel is primarily God's messenger of mercy and promise. We may question whether he blows a silver trumpet, since this idea arises from folk music and finds only indirect support in Scripture. But the announcements of Gabriel in unfolding the plans, purposes, and verdicts of God are of monumental importance.

In Scripture we gain our first glimpse of Gabriel in Daniel 8:15-16. There he announces the vision of God for the "end time." God has charged him to convey the message from the "situation room" of heaven that reveals God's plan in history. In verse 17 Gabriel says, "Understand . . . the vision belongs to (events that shall occur in) the time of the end" (AB).

Daniel, while in prayer, records Gabriel's second appearance to him: "While I was speaking in prayer, the man Gabriel, whom I had seen in the former vision, being caused to fly swiftly, came near to me and touched me about the time of the evening sacrifice" (Daniel 9:21, AB). To Daniel he said, "Understand the vision" (9:23), and then revealed to him the magnificent sequence of events at the end time. Gabriel, sketching

---

Margin:

"And it came to pass, when I, even I Daniel, had seen the vision, and sought for the meaning, then, behold, there stood before me as the appearance of a man. And I heard a man's voice between the banks of Ulai, which called, and said, Gabriel, make this man to understand the vision" (Dan. 8:15-16).

"Yea, whiles I was speaking in prayer, even the man Gabriel, whom I had seen in the vision at the beginning, being caused to fly swiftly, touched me about the time of the evening oblation. And he informed me, and talked with me, and said, O Daniel, I am now come forth to give thee skill and understanding" (Dan. 9:21-22).

"And the angel answering said unto him, I am Gabriel, that stand in the presence of God; and am sent to speak unto thee, and to show thee these glad tidings" (Luke 1:19).

"And in the sixth month the angel Gabriel was sent from God unto a city of Galilee, named Nazareth, To a virgin espoused to a man whose name was Joseph, of the house of David; and the virgin's name was Mary. And the angel came in unto her, and said, Hail, thou that art highly favored, the Lord is with thee: blessed art thou among women" (Luke 1: 26-28).

Week of DECEMBER 12

panoramically the procession of earthly kingdoms, assured Daniel that history would culminate in the return of Christ, "the prince of princes," (Daniel 8:25, AB) and conqueror of the "king of fierce countenance" (Daniel 8:23, AB). The prophetic announcement by Daniel in his prayer to God is twofold. He expressly refers to the more immediate judgment upon Israel (Daniel 9:16) and then to the awesome portent of "end time judgment" and "tribulation" which shall be for "seven years" (Daniel 9:27).

Gabriel in the New Testament

Gabriel first appears in the New Testament in Luke 1. He identifies himself to Zacharias (verse 19).

Read Luke 1:11-13 and 17. What good news did Gabriel deliver to Zacharias?

_____

Read Luke 1:26 and 30-33. What is the greatest news Gabriel has ever announced?

_____

What a message to deliver to the world through a teenage girl! What a wonderfully holy girl she must have been, to be visited by the mighty Gabriel!

Throughout all time, this divine declaration of Gabriel shall be the Magna Charta of the incarnation and the foundation stone of the world to come: God became flesh to redeem us.

What is the greatest news you've ever been privileged to deliver to someone?

_____

_____

Seraphim and Cherubim

The Seraphim

From the Bible it appears that celestial and extraterrestrial beings differ in rank and authority. The seraphim and cherubim follow in order after the archangel and angels. These may possibly define the angelic authority to which Peter refers when he speaks of Jesus, "Who is gone into heaven, and is on the right hand of God; angels and authorities and powers being made subject unto him" (1 Peter 3:22).

The word *seraphim* may come from the Hebrew root meaning "love" (though some think the word means "burning ones" or "nobles"). We find the seraphim only in Isaiah 6.

> **Read Isaiah 6:1-4. If you enjoy drawing, sketch this scene in the margin. If you are artistically challenged, answer the following:**
>
> **Where were the seraphim?** _____
>
> **What do you know about their appearance?** _____
>
> _____
>
> **What seemed to be the seraphim's job or ministry?**
>
> _____

It is an awe-inspiring sight as the worshiping prophet beholds the six-winged seraphim above the throne of the Lord. We can assume that there were several seraphim since Isaiah speaks about "each one" and "one cried unto another."

The ministry of the seraphim is to praise the name and character of God in heaven. Their ministry relates directly to God and His heavenly throne, because they are positioned above the throne—unlike the cherubim, who are beside it. Students of the Bible have not always agreed

Week of DECEMBER 12

on the duties of the seraphim, but we know one thing: they are constantly glorifying God.

Read Isaiah 6:5-7. How else can God use seraphim?

_____

These seraphim, which God used to clean and purify His servant, were indescribably beautiful. "With two [wings] he covered his face, and with two he covered his feet, and with two he did fly" (implying that some angelic beings fly). The Scriptures do not, however, support the common belief that all angels have wings. The traditional concept of angels with wings is drawn from their ability to move instantaneously and with unlimited speed from place to place, and wings were thought to permit such limitless movement. But here in Isaiah 6 only two of the seraphim's wings were employed for flying.

The Cherubim

Cherubim are real and they are powerful. But the cherubim in the Bible were often symbolic of heavenly things. God directed that they be incorporated into the design of the Ark of the Covenant and the Tabernacle. Solomon's temple also utilized cherubim in its decoration. They had wings, feet, and hands. Ezekiel 10 pictures the cherubim in detail as having not only wings and hands, but being "full of eyes," encompassed by "wheels within wheels."

But Ezekiel sounds a somber note in chapter 10 also, and the cherubim provide the clue. The prophet presents his vision that prophesies the destruction of Jerusalem. In Ezekiel 9:3, the Lord has descended from His throne above the cherubim to the threshold of the temple, while in 10:1 He returns again to take His seat above them. In the calm before the storm, we see the cherubim stationed on the south side of the sanctuary. Being stationed in position toward the city, they witness the beginning of the gradual withdrawal of God's glory from Jerusalem. The fluttering of their wings indicates immensely important events to follow (10:5). Then the cherubim rise up in preparation for the departure.

While Ezekiel 10 is difficult to understand, one point comes across clearly. The cherubim have to do with the glory of God. This chapter is

If you desire to dig deeper ...

Carefully read Ezekiel 10 specifically to gain deeper understanding of cherubim.

Record your notes below.

one of the most mysterious and yet descriptive passages of the glory of God to be found in the Bible, and it involves angelic beings. It should be read carefully and prayerfully. The reader gets a sense of God's greatness and glory as in few other passages in the Bible.

Read the following Scriptures. Draw a line from the reference to the insight it gives about cherubim.

Genesis 3:24	**Cherubim flank God's throne.**
Exodus 25:18-22	**Cherubim guard the tree of life.**
Psalm 80:1; 99:1	**Cherubim designs guarded the mercy seat in the Tabernacle.**

While the seraphim and the cherubim belong to different orders and are surrounded by much mystery in Scripture, they share one thing. They constantly glorify God. God's glory will not be denied, and every heavenly being gives silent or vocal testimony to the splendor of God.

The cherubim did more than guard the most holy place from those who had no right of access to God. They also assured the right of the high priest to enter the holy place with blood as the mediator with God on behalf of the people. He, and he alone, was permitted to enter into the inner sanctuary of the Lord. By right of redemption and in accordance with the position of believers, each true child of God now has direct access as a believer-priest to the presence of God through Jesus. Cherubim will not refuse the humblest Christian access to the throne. They assure us that we can come boldly—because of Christ's work on the cross! The veil in the temple has been rent or torn in two. The inner sanctuary of God's throne is always open to those who have repented of sin and trusted Christ as Savior.

Read the description of cherubim in Ezekiel 10:12,14,21. What word best describes your thoughts about this heavenly creature?

Creepy   Beautiful   Powerful   Indescribable

What do these awesome creatures do when you, as a believer, approach God's throne?

Week of DECEMBER 12

Angelic Spectators

How would you live if you knew you were being watched all the time, not only by your parents, wife, husband, or children, but by the heavenly host?
❑ No different than I'm living now.
❑ Always watching over my shoulder fearfully.
❑ I'd be more careful about what I said.
❑ I'd live more confidently

The Bible teaches in 1 Corinthians 4:9 that angels are watching us. Paul says we are a "spectacle" to them. The word referred to the arenas where first-century crowds went to see animals killed for sport, men battle to the death, and, later, Christians torn apart by lions. In using the word *spectacle,* Paul is picturing this world as one vast arena. All true Christians participate in this great drama as they seek to obey Christ since this throws them into severe conflict with the forces of evil, who are bent on humiliating them.

As God's angels have watched the drama of this age unfolding they have seen the Christian church established and expand around the world. They miss nothing as they watch the movements of time, "To the intent that now unto the principalities and powers in heavenly places might be known by the church the manifold wisdom of God" (Ephesians 3:10). The word "now" actually covers the vast expanse of this church age. Angel hosts have witnessed the formation of the church of Christ Jesus, and have watched the walk of each believer as the Lord worked His grace, love, and power into each life. The angels are observing firsthand the building of the body of the true church in all places of His dominion this very hour.

"For I think that God hath set forth us the apostles last, as it were appointed to death: for we are made a spectacle unto the world, and to angels, and to men" (1 Cor. 4:9, KJV).

What do you think the angels are thinking as they watch the church live in the world's arena?

_____

What about you? Do the angels: (check one)
❑ Observe you standing fast in the faith and walking in righteousness?   OR
❑ Wonder at your lack of commitment?

If you desire to dig deeper ...

**Read the following verses and identify the judgment that followed each trumpet blast by an angel:
Revelation 8:7-13; 9:1-4, 13-15; 11:15-19.**

Our certainty that angels right now witness how we are walking through life should mightily influence the decisions we make. God is watching, and His angels are interested spectators too. *The Amplified Bible* expresses 1 Corinthians 4:9 this way: "God has made an exhibit of us . . . a show in the world's amphitheater—with both men and angels (as spectators)."

Read 1 Timothy 5:21. Who was constantly watching how Timothy served the Savior and lived the Christian life? _____

The charge to live righteously in this present world sobers us when we realize that the walk and warfare of Christians is the primary concern of heaven and its angelic hosts. What fact could provide a greater motivation to righteous living than that? I must say to myself, "Careful, angels are watching!

God's Agents in Judgment

We often get false notions about angels from plays given by Sunday School children at Christmas. It is true that angels are ministering spirits sent to help the heirs of salvation. But just as they fulfill God's will in salvation for believers in Jesus Christ, so they are also "avengers" who use their great power to fulfill God's will in judgment.

The Bible says that throughout history angels have worked to carry out God's judgments, directing the destinies of nations disobedient to God. For example, God used angels in scattering the people of Israel because of their sins. He also used angels in bringing judgment on Sodom and Gomorrah, and eventually on Babylon and Nineveh. And one of the angels will blow the trumpet that announces impending judgment when God summons the nations to stand before Him in the last great judgment.

Scripture clearly teaches that angels will be God's emissaries to carry out His judgment against those who deliberately reject Jesus Christ and the salvation God offers through Him. While all people are sinners by nature, choice, and practice, yet it is the deliberate rejection of Jesus Christ

Week of DECEMBER 12

as Savior and Lord that causes the judgment of eternal separation from God. God has assigned angels at the end of the age to separate the sheep from the goats, the wheat from the chaff, the saved from the lost. We are not called upon to obey the voice of angels, but we are to heed and obey the Word of God and the voice of God that calls us to be reconciled to Him by faith in Jesus Christ. If not, we will have to pay the penalty of unforgiven sin.

Read Matthew 13:49-50 in the margin and underline the penalty the angels will administer to the wicked.

I am constantly astounded that God's decrees and warnings are considered so lightly in our modern world—even among Christians.

Every one of Adam's race is confronted with two ways of life: one, to eternal life; the other, to eternal death. We have seen how angels execute God's judgment on those who reject Jesus—the angels cast them into the furnace of fire. But there is a totally different judgment: It is the good and wonderful judgment unto everlasting life. God gives the angels a place in this too. He commissions them to escort each believer to heaven and to give him or her a royal welcome as he or she enters the eternal presence of God. Each of us who trusts Christ will witness the rejoicing of angelic hosts around the throne of God.

In the story of the rich man and Lazarus (Luke 16), Jesus told of a beggar who died in the faith. He had never owned many of this world's goods, but he was rich in faith that counts for eternity.

Read Luke 16:22 in the margin. Underline the reward the angels administered to Lazarus.

Here were angelic pallbearers who took his immortal spirit to the place of glory where he was to be eternally with God—the place the Bible calls "heaven."

Do you fear the judgment of God? Or do you know that Christ has taken your judgment upon Himself by His death on the cross? When you know Christ you need not fear God's judgment, for He has fully and completely purchased your salvation. Don't delay your decision for Christ, but open your heart to Him and you too will know the joy of sharing in His fellowship throughout all eternity in heaven.

"So shall it be at the end of the world: the angels shall come forth, and sever the wicked from among the just, And shall cast them into the furnace of fire" (Matt. 13:49-50, KJV).

"And it came to pass, that the beggar died, and was carried by the angels into Abraham's bosom" (Luke 16:22).

Circle the passage in either Matthew 13:49-50 or Luke 16:22 that describes the action the angels would take on your behalf if you were to die today.
Then read the inside front cover of this publication to discover how to receive salvation from eternal judgment.

Amy SUMMER

NOTES

To the Leader:

The "dig deeper" activities in the margin involve some very difficult passages of Scripture to understand. Engage in personal commentary study of these passages if you intend to use those activities in your teaching plan.

Before the Session
1. Prayerfully choose the teaching steps that will help your class explore the material in this week's lesson.
2. Prepare a chain of command poster titled "Hierarchy of Angels." You'll want to include spaces to write the titles and/or names of angels in Steps 2-5. (This poster can be very simple or detailed—choose a format that will best help your class grasp the material.)

During the Session
1. Ask learners to think of institutions of which they are a part, including family, work, and church. Ask: *Do you prefer those institutions to have a definite chain of command or to be more loosely organized with everyone being his or her own boss? Why?* OR Request participants chart on a piece of paper the chain of command of an organization to which they belong. Ask why rankings are necessary within an organization.
2. Display the "Hierarchy of Angels" poster. Ask if participants are surprised to learn there is a definite ranking of angels and why. Ask the class to state the title of the highest ranking angel. Write *archangel* at the top of the poster. (Continue recording responses on the poster throughout the discussion of angelic organization. You will not be reminded each time.) Guide the class to define *archangel*. Complete the first two activities of Day 1. Direct adults to listen for additional information about the archangel as you read aloud Revelation 12:7-8. Invite volunteers to share their insights. Invite a volunteer to read Daniel 12:1-3. Ask: *What will happen at the end time to those who, like Michael, are on God's side?* Ask someone to read Jude 8. Comment that while believers are not to revere Michael, they are to respect him. Encourage adults to take this study of angels seriously because God does!
3. Request someone name the next ranking below archangel as identified by Billy Graham. Ask the class to name the most prominent angel and define his name (beginning of Day 2). Explain Gabriel delivered messages of understanding and good news. Guide the class to explore

Week of DECEMBER 12

what Gabriel helped Daniel understand in Daniel 8:19-26. Remark that although Gabriel's comments might have been frightening, he also delivered good news to Daniel. Request adults read silently Daniel 9:21-23 and identify the good news. Discuss the second activity of Day 2 to discover additional good news Gabriel was privileged to announce. Direct adults to read silently Luke 1:12-13 and 29-30. Ask if they would have had a similar response to Gabriel's appearance and why. Discuss times when adults might need to hear the good news that they don't need to be afraid.

4. Request someone name the next celestial being in the angelic hierarchy. Write *Seraphim* on the poster. Use the text and first two activities in Day 3 to gain an understanding into seraphim. Invite someone to read Isaiah 6:8. Ask what the encounter with the seraphim prepared Isaiah to do and how that reinforces the truth of Hebrews 1:14. (Draw attention to the poster of Hebrews 1:14 displayed last week.)

5. Write *Cherubim* on the angelic hierarchy poster. Ask what most people think of when they hear the word *cherub*. Read aloud Ezekiel 10:12,14,21 and ask how closely the biblical cherubim resemble the popular concept. Acknowledge this order of angels is difficult to understand but their role is quite simple. Challenge participants to state a common theme of the three insights about cherubim listed in the third activity of Day 3. (They are guardians.) Explain that the cherubim guard God's glory. Encourage participants and remind them that believers also need to be ever watchful (referring to the cherubim's multiple eyes and faces) to glorify God.

6. Ask: *When was the last time you made a spectacle of yourself?* Invite someone to read 1 Corinthians 4:9. Explain the meaning of that verse. Discuss the first activity and the first question of the second activity in Day 4.

7. Ask how often angels are portrayed as agents of judgment in the entertainment media. Comment that the world likes to see angels as messengers of peace and love, but angels also are stern deliverers of judgment. Read aloud Isaiah 37:36-37. Request participants silently read Isaiah 37:21-24 to discover the reason for the judgment they bring. Ask what other kind of judgment angels deliver. (everlasting life to believers.) Encourage participants to speak with you if they are uncertain which judgment they will face.

NOTES

Billy GRAHAM

Angels, the Good News, and the Birth of Jesus

day One

The Angel and Zacharias

The birth of John the Baptist was dynamically connected with the "evangel," a term meaning the gospel, the good news of God's salvation in Jesus Christ.

Read Luke 1:5-7. Describe John the Baptist's parents, Zacharias and Elizabeth, in terms of their:

Age: _____

Family situation: _____

Relationship with God: _____

When the angel appeared to Zacharias to announce the good news that Elizabeth would, despite her age, give birth to a son, his words were immersed in the evangel. The angel predicted John's ministry: "Many of the children of Israel shall he turn to the Lord their God" (Luke 1:16). Moreover John was "to make ready a people prepared for the Lord" (verse 17).

How great the message of the angel was and how seriously Zacharias regarded it can be seen from events some months later. Zacharias lost his ability to speak following the angel's visit; he did not regain it until the birth of John. At that time his tongue was loosed and he was filled with the Holy Spirit. His thinking—during the long months while Elizabeth awaited the birth of the baby—now burst out in his first words, which reflect the angel's visit and concern for the evangel.

Week of DECEMBER 19

Read Luke 1:68-79. What is the overriding theme of Zacharias' song?
- ❑ Look at my beautiful son!
- ❑ God's salvation
- ❑ I have my voice back!

What did Zacharias say his son would do? _____
_____

Now that was really a message! And all of it rises from the visit of the angel, who told Zacharias about God's intention for John. Notice especially that the angel came not simply to announce the birth of John but to make it clear that John was to live his life as the forerunner of the Messiah and as one who would bring the knowledge of salvation and the remission of sins to his fellow Israelites.

Who prepared you to receive the good news of Jesus? _____ **Thank God for this person.**
Who are you preparing to receive the good news of God's salvation? _____

The Angel, Mary, and Joseph

The announcement to Mary that she was to be the mother of Jesus was made by no ordinary angel. It was made by Gabriel. And it was connected with the evangel or good news. This was true both of the words Gabriel spoke and of the words Mary spoke while she was pregnant and looking toward the birth of her son. The angel told Mary that Jesus would be the Son of the Highest, that He would inherit the throne of His father David, that He would reign over the house of Jacob forever, and that it would be an everlasting kingdom. This was something far different from anything promised anyone else in Scripture. This was not promised to Abraham, or David, or Solomon. Only Jesus' name is connected with these promises, and all of them are inextricably connected with both personal and national salvation.

> **Mary's Song**
> (Luke 1:46-55, HCSB)
>
> "My soul proclaims the greatness of the Lord, and my spirit has rejoiced in God my Savior, because He has looked with favor on the humble condition of His slave. Surely, from now on all generations will call me blessed, because the Mighty One has done great things for me, and His name is holy. His mercy is from generation to generation on those who fear Him. He has done a mighty deed with His arm; He has scattered the proud because of the thoughts of their hearts; He has toppled the mighty from their thrones and exalted the lowly. He has satisfied the hungry with good things and sent the rich away empty. He has helped His servant Israel, mindful of His mercy, just as He spoke to our ancestors, to Abraham and his descendants forever."

After Mary became pregnant she visited Elizabeth and sang one of the sweetest songs known to literature.

Read Mary's song in the margin. Underline what she called God.

Mary makes evident that she had grasped what the angel told her. Here was the news that Mary herself needed a Savior, and that she had found Him. The very baby who was encased in her womb would one day offer Himself as a propitiation for her and for all mankind. And that baby in her womb was God Almighty who had humbled Himself in order to dwell among us in the flesh.

Indeed she cried out that God's "mercy is on them that fear him from generation to generation." What is this but the glorious evangel, gospel, that God was in Christ reconciling the world to Himself? And this was the message Gabriel brought to Mary. He could not preach it himself, but he could bear witness to the gospel that was to be preached by Jesus Christ and His followers through all ages.

Joseph, the husband of Mary, was caught up in a seemingly abysmal situation. He was legally engaged to a girl who was pregnant. He knew he was not the father because they had not yet consummated their forthcoming marriage. Yet Mary was apparently guilty of adultery under Jewish law, unless Joseph was willing to believe her story that the Holy Spirit had come upon her, and that she had never engaged in sexual relations with a man. As the innocent party, Joseph was thinking seriously of putting Mary away according to the custom of that day.

Read Matthew 1:20-24. Number the events below in the order they occur in this passage.
___ **Joseph married Mary.**
___ **The angel told Joseph Mary's Son would save people from their sins.**
___ **Joseph named the baby Jesus.**
___ **An angel appeared to Joseph.**

Here was the gospel in all of its beauty, simplicity, and purity. According to the witness of the angel, sins can be forgiven. There is someone who can forgive sins. This is Jesus the Christ. The Savior has a people about whom

Week of **DECEMBER 19**

He is concerned and guarantees that their sins will be forgiven. In the midst of the wonder of the incarnation we should not overlook the fact that the angel was here bearing witness to the evangel, the gospel. Jesus was not coming simply as God. He was coming as Redeemer and Savior to make human beings right with His Father and to assure them of the gift of everlasting life.

> **Have you noticed that none of those who had encounters with angels mentioned the angels again? Their focus wasn't on the messenger, but on praising God for His wonderful message! As a messenger of the gospel do you seek to:**
> ❑ **Draw attention to yourself?   OR**
> ❑ **Draw attention to the glory of the gospel?**

The Angel and the Shepherds

Does it not seem mysterious that God brought the first message of the birth of Jesus to ordinary people rather than to princes and kings? In this instance, God spoke through His holy angel to the shepherds who were keeping sheep in the fields. This was a lowly occupation, so shepherds were not well educated. But Mary in her song, the Magnificat, tells us the true story: "He hath put down the mighty from their seats, and exalted them of low degree. He hath filled the hungry with good things, and the rich he hath sent empty away" (Luke 1:52-53).

> **Read Luke 2:8-11. Complete the sentences to state the two-fold message of the angel to the shepherds.**
>
> **First he told them not to** _____
>
> **Then he told them** _____

Over and over again the presence of angels was frightening to those to whom they came. But unless they came in judgment, the angels spoke a word of reassurance. They calmed the people to whom they came. This tells us that the appearance of angels is awe-inspiring, something about them awakening fear in the human heart. They represent a presence that has greatness and sends a chill down the spine. But when the angel had quieted the fears of the shepherds, he brought this message, one forever to be connected with the evangel: "For behold I bring you good tidings of great joy, which shall be to all people. For unto you is born this day in the city of David a Savior, which is Christ the Lord" (Luke 2:10-11).

I could preach a dozen sermons on those two verses for they contain so many important theological themes. But note once more that the angel does not preach the gospel. Rather, he witnesses to it and demonstrates again the overwhelming concern angels have for it.

What did the angel say? First, he brought good tidings, not bad ones. The shepherds already knew the bad news—the human race had sinned and was lost. But the angel had come to tell them that God was doing something about their lostness. And he pointed out that the good news was not simply for the people of one nation but for the whole world. Isaiah said, "The God of the whole earth shall he be called" (Isaiah 54:5). The angel told the shepherds that the good tidings were for all people.

The good tidings were that the Savior had come. Human beings needed somebody who could bring them back into fellowship with God, because the blood of bulls and goats could not do this in any permanent way. But the blood of the Savior could. The angel message was that God had come, redemption was possible, the Lord had visited His people with salvation. What a testimony to the evangel this was.

> "The angel message was that God had come, redemption was possible, the Lord had visited His people with salvation."
> —Billy Graham

Read Luke 2:13-14.

What further validated the angel's message? _____

_____

Record what the angels proclaimed. _____

_____

Week of DECEMBER 19

Angel Ministries in Jesus' Life

Angels and Jesus' Temptations in the Wilderness

If you desire to dig deeper ...

Read about the temptation of Jesus in Matthew 4:1-11. Record below each of Satan's temptations and the Scripture Jesus used to counter each temptation.

Perhaps the most difficult period in the life of Jesus before His crucifixion was His temptation by the devil in the wilderness. After He had fasted forty days and nights, Satan tried to break Him down. In Christ's weakened human condition, Satan began his attack, seeing this as his greatest opportunity to defeat the program of God in the world since his victory in the Garden of Eden. He was out to shipwreck the hope of the human race. Wishing to prevent the salvation of sinners, Satan struck at the moment when Christ's physical weakness made Him most susceptible to temptation. Satan always directs his sharpest attack at his victim's weakest point. He knows where the Achilles heel may be, and he does not fail to strike at the opportune time.

Three times Satan attempted to defeat Jesus. Three times Jesus quoted Scripture, and three times Satan went down to defeat.

> **Read Matthew 4:11. What happened after Satan left Jesus? (circle one)**
> - **Jesus took a nap**
> - **Angels came and ministered to Jesus**
> - **Jesus' disciples brought Him food**

The angels didn't come to help Jesus resist Satan as they help us, for Jesus did that by Himself, but to help Him after the battle was won. The angels "ministered" to Jesus. The Greek word *diakoneo* says it well, for they served Him as a deacon would serve. Angelic ambassadors supported, strengthened, and sustained Jesus in that trying hour.

The Angel with Jesus in the Garden of Gethsemane

The night before His crucifixion Jesus was in the Garden of Gethsemane. Only a short time later He was to be seized by the soldiers, betrayed by Judas Iscariot, set before the rulers, beaten, and at last crucified. Before He was hung on the cross He went through the terrible agony in the Garden that made Him sweat, as it were, drops of blood. It was in this situation that the Son of Man needed inner strength to face what no other being in heaven, hell, or earth had ever known. In fact, He was to face what no created being could have faced and gone through in victory. He was about to take upon Himself the sins of all mankind. He was to become sin for us.

Read Luke 22:39-46. Circle who provided strength for Jesus when He most needed it. Draw a star next the one(s) that best represent your devotion to Jesus.

Peter, James, and John   **An angel**

Jesus had taken Peter, James, and John with Him to the Garden. They could have provided Him with reinforcement and encouragement, but instead they fell asleep. The Son of Man was all alone. He prayed, "Father, if thou be willing, remove this cup from me: nevertheless not my will, but thine, be done" (Luke 22:42). Then it was at that crucial moment that the angel came to assist Him, "strengthening Him." The Greek word for "strengthening" is *eniskuo*, which means to make strong inwardly. Where the disciples of the Lord Jesus had failed to share His agony, as they slept the angel came to help.

Angels Waiting at the Cross

The tragedy of sin reached its crescendo when God in Christ became sin. At this point He was offering Himself as the sacrifice required by the justice of God if human beings were to be redeemed. At this moment Satan was ready to try his master stroke. If he could get Christ to come down from the cross, and if Christ allowed the mockery of the crowd to shame or anger Him, then the plan of salvation would be jeopardized. Again and again they shouted, "If thou be the Son of God, come down

Week of DECEMBER 19

from the cross" (Matthew 27:40). Jesus knew He could come down if He chose; He knew He could get help from more than twelve legions of angels who hovered about with drawn swords.

Yet for our salvation He stayed there. The angels would have come to the cross to rescue the King of kings, but because of His love for the human race and because He knew it was only through His death that we could be saved, He refused to call for their help. The angels were under orders not to intervene at this terrible, holy moment. Even the angels could not minister to the Son of God at Calvary. He died alone to take the full death penalty you and I deserved.

We can never plumb the depths of sin, or sense how terrible human sin is, until we go to the cross and see that it was "sin" that caused the Son of God to be crucified. The ravages of war, the tragedy of suicide, the agony of the poverty-stricken, the suffering and irony of the rejected of our society, the blood of the accident victim, the terror of rape and mugging victims of our generation—these all speak as with a single voice of the degradation that besets the human race at this hour. But no sin has been committed in the world today that can compare with the full cup of the universe's sin that brought Jesus to the cross. The question hurled toward heaven throughout the ages has been, "Who is He and why does He die?" The answer comes back, "This is My only begotten Son, dying not only for your sins but for the sins of the whole world." To you sin may be a small thing; to God it is a great and awful thing. It is the second largest thing in the world; only the love of God is greater.

When we comprehend the great price God was willing to pay for the redemption of mankind, we only then begin to see that something is horribly wrong with the human race. It must have a Savior, or it is doomed! Sin cost God His very best. Is it any wonder that the angels veiled their faces, that they were silent in their consternation as they witnessed the outworking of God's plan? How inconceivable it must have seemed to them, when they considered the fearful depravity of sin, that Jesus should shoulder it all. But they were soon to unveil their faces and offer their praises again. A light was kindled that day at Calvary. The cross blazed with the glory of God as the most terrible darkness was shattered by the light of salvation. Satan's depraved legions were defeated and they could no longer keep all humanity in darkness and defeat.

Read aloud or sing the hymn "Ten Thousand Angels" by Ray Overholt. Thank your Savior for His sacrifice on your behalf.

They bound the hands of Jesus in the garden where He prayed;
They led Him thro' the streets in shame.
They spat upon the Savior so pure and free from sin;
They said, "Crucify Him; He's to blame."
To the howling mob He yielded; He did not for mercy cry.
The cross of shame He took alone.
And when He cried, "It's finished," He gave Himself to die;
Salvation's wondrous plan was done.

He could have called ten thousand angels
To destroy the world and set Him free.
He could have called ten thousand angels,
But He died alone, for you and me.[1]

day Five

The Angels at Jesus' Resurrection and Ascension

Conduct a comparison study of the role of angels at Jesus' resurrection as recounted in all four gospels. Read the following passages and make notes under the headings in the margin.

Matthew 28:1-7   **Mark 16:1-7**
Luke 24:1-7   **John 20:10-13**

On the third day after His death the Bible says, "And behold there was a great earthquake; for the angel of the Lord descended from heaven, and came and rolled back the stone from the door, and sat upon it. His coun-

Week of DECEMBER 19

tenance was like lightning, and his raiment white as snow: And for fear of him the keepers did shake, and became as dead men" (Matthew 28:2-4).

Though some Bible students have tried to estimate how much this stone weighed, we need not speculate because Jesus could have come out of that tomb whether the stone was there or not. The Bible mentions it so that generations to come can know something of the tremendous miracle of resurrection that took place. I have often wondered what those guards must have thought when, against the brightness of the rising sun, they saw the angel rolling away the gigantic boulder with possibly the lightest touch of his finger! The guards, though heavily armed, were paralyzed with fear.

As Mary looked into the tomb she saw "two angels in white sitting, the one at the head, and the other at the feet, where the body of Jesus had lain" (John 20:11, 12). Then one of the angels who was sitting outside the tomb proclaimed the greatest message the world has ever heard: "He is not here, but is risen" (Luke 24:6). Those few words changed the history of the universe. Darkness and despair died; hope and anticipation were born in people's hearts.

We find the story of the ascension of Jesus in Acts 1. Verse 9 says, "And when he had spoken these things, while they beheld, he was taken up; and a cloud received him out of their sight." The watching disciples were sad and despondent. Tears filled their eyes. But again two angels, looking like men and dressed in white raiment, appeared and said, "Ye men of Galilee, why stand ye gazing up into heaven? This same Jesus, which is taken up from you into heaven, shall so come in like manner as ye have seen him go into heaven" (Acts 1:11). Thus when the resurrected Lord of glory ascended to be seated at the Father's right hand, angels assured the early disciples that Christ would return in person with an angelic host.

Number of angels:

Location of the angels:

What the angels said:

What the angels did:

State the two momentous declarations the angels made about Jesus at His resurrection and ascension.

He is _____

He will _____

Pray for the opportunity and obedience to share these great truths with someone this week.

[1]"Ten Thousand Angels" by Ray Overholt. © Copyright 1959. Renewed 1987 Lillenas Publishing Company (admin. by The Copyright Company). All rights reserved. Used by permission.

leader Guide

NOTES

To the Leader:

You will be studying Scriptures that are familiar to most participants. Pray for insight to present the beauty of the Christmas story in a new way so participants will not only appreciate the role angels played throughout Jesus' life, but will also gain new insight into the glory of His coming. You may choose to focus on the first three days of material, but don't neglect the additional material—you want to be certain participants also grasp the glory of Jesus' coming again!

Before the Session

1. You won't have time to complete all the teaching steps. Prayerfully choose suggestions that will help your class explore the material you feel most needs to be covered during the class session.
2. Obtain a recording of the song "Mary Did You Know?"

During the Session

1. Invite volunteers to share their favorite Christmas memories. Remark that today you will study what surely became favorite memories of those persons involved in the first Christmas. OR Challenge participants to name as many TV Christmas specials that involve angels as they can. Ask: *What did the angels do in those shows? Why do angels seem to surge in popularity in December?* Remark that in today's lesson learners will see how angels figured prominently in the first Christmas.

2. Lead the class to complete the first activity of Day 1. Ask which characteristic of Zacharias and Elizabeth made them most in need of a miracle. Invite someone to read Luke 1:11-14. Ask if the angel brought about the miracle. Read Luke 1:18 and ask whether Zacharias was questioning whether the angel was real or whether he was telling the truth. Inquire as to why that would make a difference in the angel's response. Note that though the angel was kind in verse 13, he became quite stern with Zacharias. Read Luke 1:19-20. Briefly summarize verses 21-25, 39-45, and 57-66. Ask what participants think might have been Zacharias's and Elizabeth's favorite memories from this time. Complete the second activity of Day 1.

3. If possible, request a woman read Luke 1:26-38 and a man read Matthew 1:18-25. Ask participants to state what they think would be Mary and Joseph's favorite memories of the time they first heard of their roles in the birth of God's Son. Ask whether participants think Mary was fully aware of what it meant for her Son to be her Savior. If possible, play a recording of "Mary Did You Know?"

Week of DECEMBER 19

4. Invite someone to read Luke 2:8-14. Invite another person to read the quotation in the margin in Day 3. Inquire: *Is this only a message for angels to deliver? How can we follow the angel's example in Luke 2:8-12 to share this message?* Comment that this message should lead believers into an outburst of praise. Invite someone to read Luke 2:16-20. Ask what participants think was the shepherd's favorite memory of that night. Read the last activity of Day 2 and challenge participants to quietly consider the personal question.

5. Remark that angels didn't just announce Jesus' birth and disappear. Matthew 4:11 and Luke 22:43 depict angels strengthening Jesus near the beginning and end of His earthly ministry. Request volunteers read those verses. Inquire: *What does it say to you that Jesus needed the ministry of angels?* Invite volunteers to share times they believe that they have been strengthened or sustained by angels. If no one shares, comment that they may have received the ministry of angels but just not recognized it (Heb. 13:2). Exhort participants that if they know of times angels have helped them, they should always give God the glory for sending that angel to help. As in the previous lessons, refer to the poster of Hebrews 1:14. Request someone read Matthew 26:52-54. Ask how it makes participants feel to know Jesus refused to call on willing angels to deliver Him in His darkest hour.

6. Complete the first activity of Day 5. Organize the class into several groups. Direct each group to write a letter from one of the guards at the tomb to his mother telling her what happened that Sunday morning. Allow groups to share their letters. Invite someone to read Acts 1:7-11. Ask what participants think was the disciples' clearest memory of Christ's ascension.

7. Comment that each person you studied today had different memories of their encounters with angels. Remark that it is OK if participants don't have memories of angelic encounters because the truth of Christ's birth, death, and resurrection means they can have the reality of a daily encounter with the Savior Himself. That's the message the angels were privileged to deliver. Now believers have the privilege to deliver that good news as well. Encourage participants to do so this week by identifying the name of someone with whom they will share the evangel, the good news.

8. Close in prayer.

NOTES

Angels: Now and in the Future

day One

Angels Stand Ready to Help

The enemies of Christ who attack us incessantly would often be thwarted if we could grasp God's assurance that His mighty angels are always nearby, ready to help. Tragically, most Christians have failed to accept this fact so frequently expressed in the Bible.

God's angels often protect His servants from potential enemies. Consider 2 Kings 6:14-17. The king of Syria had dispatched his army to Dothan, learning that Elisha the prophet was there.

> **Read 2 Kings 6:14-17 and fill in the blanks to complete the sentences.**
>
> **Elisha's servant saw _____ surrounding the city.**
>
> **Elisha saw _____ surrounding the city.**
>
> **Do you view your circumstances with eyes like:
> Elisha's servant?   OR   Elisha? (Circle one)**

This passage has been one of the great assurances and comforts to me in my ministry.

The angels minister to God's servants in time of hardship and danger. We find another outstanding illustration of this in Acts 27:23-25. Paul, on his way to Rome, faced shipwreck with more than two hundred others

Week of DECEMBER 26

on board. Speaking to the fear-ridden crew he said, "Last night an angel of the God whose I am and whom I serve, stood beside me and said, 'Do not be afraid, Paul. You must stand trial before Caesar; and God has graciously given you the lives of all who sail with you'" (verses 23-24, NIV).

Some believe strongly that each Christian may have his own guardian angel assigned to watch over him or her.

Read Matthew 18:10 in the margin. When might this guardianship possibly begin? (check one)
❏ When the person receives Christ.
❏ When the person is an infant.
❏ When the person asks for it.
❏ Other: _____

> "See that you do not look down on one of these little ones. For I tell you that their angels in heaven always see the face of my Father in heaven" (Matt. 18:10, NIV).

The most important characteristic of angels is not that they have power to exercise control over our lives, or that they are beautiful, but that they work on our behalf. They are motivated by an inexhaustible love for God and are jealous to see that the will of God in Jesus Christ is fulfilled in us.

David says of angels, "He who dwelleth in the secret place of the Most High shall abide under the shadow of the Almighty. . . . For he shall give his angels charge over thee, to keep thee in all thy ways. They shall bear thee up . . . lest thou dash thy foot against a stone" (Psalm 91:1,11-12).

day Two

Angels Protect and Deliver Us

Every true believer in Christ should be encouraged and strengthened! Angels are watching; they mark our path. They superintend the events of our lives and protect the interest of the Lord God, always working to promote His plans and to bring about His highest will for us. Angels are interested spectators and mark all we do, "for we are made a spectacle unto the world, and to angels, and to men" (1 Corinthians 4:9). God assigns angelic powers to watch over us.

It is ironic that Abraham, after having scaled such glorious heights of faith, should have capitulated to his wife's conniving and scolding and to the custom of that day to father a child by Hagar, Sarah's maid. And it is ironic that Sarah his wife should have been so jealous that when their own son, Isaac, was born years later, she wanted to get rid of both Hagar and the earlier child, Ishmael. So Abraham's self-indulgence led to sorrow and he thrust Hagar out of his home.

Nonetheless, God sent His angel to minister to Hagar. "And the angel of the Lord found her by a fountain of water in the wilderness, by the fountain in the way to Shur" (Genesis 16:7). The angel spoke as an oracle of God, turning her mind away from the injury of the past with a promise of what she might expect if she placed her faith in God. This God is the God not only of Israel but the God of the Arab as well (for the Arabs come from the stock of Ishmael). The very name of her son, Ishmael, meaning "God hears," was a sustaining one. God promised that the seed of Ishmael would multiply, and that his destiny would be great on the earth as he now undertook the restless pilgrimage that was to characterize his descendants. The angel of the Lord revealed himself as the protector of Hagar and Ishmael. Hagar in awe exclaimed, "Thou God seest me" (Genesis 16:13), or as it may be better translated, "I have seen Thou who seest all and who sees me."

> **How do you respond to the truth that God hears and sees you at all times? (check all that apply)**
> ❏ **It scares me.**
> ❏ **Like Hagar, I'm in awe.**
> ❏ **I feel protected.**
> ❏ **It makes me feel vulnerable.**

Psalm 34:7 underscores the teaching that angels protect and deliver us, "The angel of the Lord encampeth round about those who fear him, and delivereth them."

A classic example of the protective agency of angels is found in Acts 12:5-11. Peter was bound in prison awaiting execution. James, the brother of John, had been killed already, and there was little reason to suppose that Peter would escape the executioner's ax. The magistrates intended to put him to death as a favor to those who opposed the gospel and the works of God. Surely the believers had prayed for James, but God had chosen to deliver him through death. Now the church was praying for Peter.

Week of DECEMBER 26

Read Acts 12:1-11.
Write the correct number in the blanks.

Peter was guarded by _____ soldiers and secured with _____ chains.

What happened to Peter's chains? _____

How did Peter get past the guards? _____

How did Peter get through the iron gate of the prison? _____

The Scriptures are full of dramatic evidences of the protective care of angels in their earthly service to the people of God. Paul admonished Christians to put on all the armor of God that they may stand firmly in the face of evil (Ephesians 6:10-12). Our struggle is not against flesh and blood (physical powers alone) but against the spiritual (superhuman) forces of wickedness in heavenly spheres. Satan, the prince of the power of the air, promotes a "religion" but not true faith; he promotes false prophets. So the powers of light and darkness are locked in intense conflict. Thank God for the angelic forces that fight off the works of darkness. Angels never minister selfishly; they serve so that all glory may be given to God as believers are strengthened.

The great majority of Christians can recall some incident in which their lives, in times of critical danger, have been miraculously preserved—a near car wreck or a fierce temptation. Though they may have seen no angels, their presence could explain why tragedy was averted. We should always be grateful for the goodness of God, who uses these wonderful friends called angels to protect us. Evidence from Scripture as well as personal experience confirms to us that individual guardian, guiding angels attend at least some of our ways and hover protectively over our lives.

Can you name some time or times when you feel you were protected by the guardianship of angels?

_____

_____

day Three

Angels Are With Us at Death

Do you fear your own death? ❑ Yes ❑ No

If Yes, what do you fear most? _____

Do you associate angels with your death? _____

Why? How? _____

Death is not natural, for man was created to live and not to die. It is the result of God's judgment because of man's sin and rebellion. Without God's grace through Christ, it is a gruesome spectacle. I have stood at the bedside of people dying without Christ; it was a terrible experience. I have stood at the bedside of those who were dying in Christ; it was a glorious experience. Death for the Christian cuts the cord that holds us captive in this present evil world so that angels may transport believers to their heavenly inheritance.

Death is robbed of much of its terror for the true believer, but we still need God's protection as we take that last journey. At the moment of death the spirit departs from the body and moves through the atmosphere. But the Scripture teaches us that the devil lurks there. He is "the prince of the power of the air" (Ephesians 2:2). If the eyes of our understanding were opened, we would probably see the air filled with demons, the enemies of Christ. If Satan could hinder the angel of Daniel 10 for three weeks on his mission to earth (Daniel 10:12-13), we can imagine the opposition a Christian may encounter at death.

But Christ on Calvary cleared a road through Satan's kingdom. When Christ came to earth, He had to pass through the devil's territory and open up a beachhead here. That is one reason He was accompanied by a host of angels when He came (Luke 2:8-14). And this is why holy angels will accompany Him when He comes again (Matthew 16:27). Till then, the moment of death is Satan's final opportunity to attack the true believer; but God has sent His angels to guard us at that time.

Week of DECEMBER 26

In telling the story in Luke 16 Jesus says that the beggar was "carried by the angels" (Luke 16:22). He was not only escorted; he was carried! What an experience that must have been for Lazarus! He had lain begging at the gate of the rich man until his death, but then suddenly he found himself carried by the mighty angels of God!

Once I stood in London to watch Queen Elizabeth return from an overseas trip. I saw the parade of dignitaries, the marching bands, the crack troops, the waving flags. I saw all the splendor that accompanies the homecoming of a queen. However, that was nothing compared to the homecoming of a true believer who has said good-bye here to all of the suffering of this life and been immediately surrounded by angels who carry him or her upward to the glorious welcome awaiting the redeemed in heaven.

The Christian should never consider death a tragedy. Rather he should see it as angels do: They realize that joy should mark the journey from time to eternity. The way to life is by the valley of death, but the road is marked with victory all the way. Angels revel in the power of the resurrection of Jesus, which assures us of our resurrection and guarantees us a safe passage to heaven. I believe that death can be beautiful. I have come to look forward to it, to anticipate it with joy and expectation.

David said, "Even though I walk through the valley of the shadow of death, I will fear no evil, for you are with me" (Psalm 23:4, NIV). But you may be filled with dread at the thought of death. Just remember that at one moment you may be suffering, but in another moment, you will be instantly transformed into the glorious likeness of our Savior. The wonders, beauties, splendor, and grandeur of heaven will be yours. You will be surrounded by these heavenly messengers sent by God to bring you home where you may rest from your labors, though the honor of your works will follow you (Revelation 14:13).

Read Psalm 116:15 in the margin. How does this verse help you view your death with anticipation rather than dread?

"Precious in the sight of the Lord is the death of his saints" (Ps. 116:15).

_____

_____

day Four

Angels and the Final Victory

Angels Will Accompany Christ When He Returns

Angels figure prominently in the prophetic plan of God that continues on into the future events of Bible prophecy. Just as millions of angels participated in the dazzling show when the morning stars sang together at creation, so will the innumerable hosts of heaven help bring to pass God's prophetic declarations.

When God decrees it, Satan (Lucifer) will be removed from the world of disorder so God can establish righteousness everywhere, and a true theocracy. Not until that event takes place will the human race know perfect peace on earth. Paul tells us in Romans 8 that the whole creation groans and travails as it awaits the day of Christ's victory.

In every age, true believers have asked, "Will this conflict of the ages ever end?" Yes, someday Satan and his demons will go down in defeat. The Bible declares that righteousness will eventually triumph, Utopia will come to earth, the kingdom of God will ultimately prevail. In bringing all this about angels will have a prominent part. God will use the angels to merge time into eternity.

But the Age of Utopia will be preceded by unparalleled events of suffering for the human race—totalitarianism, poverty, disease, earthquakes, moral collapse, war—until men's hearts will fail them for fear (Luke 21:9-26). Even as in the beginning of time angelic forces waged war in heaven (Revelation 12:7-9), so in the very last days angels will wage still another war; Satan will make his last stand. The Book of Revelation, from chapter 4 to 19, gives us a picture of judgments to befall the earth such as the world has never known. Angels will be involved in all of these judgments. But after these terrifying events, Christ will come with His holy angels to set up His kingdom.

We are not left in doubt about who will ultimately triumph. Time after time Jesus has assured us that He and the angels would be victorious (Matthew 13:41-42). "When the Son of man shall come in his glory,

Week of DECEMBER 26

and all the holy angels with him, then shall he sit upon the throne of his glory" (Matthew 25:31). The apostle Paul wrote, "The Lord Jesus shall be revealed from heaven with his mighty angels in flaming fire" (2 Thessalonians 1:7-8). It will be a victorious day for the universe, and especially planet earth, when the devil and his fallen angels are thrown into the lake of fire, never again to tempt and destroy man.

Angels Will Gather God's Elect

Linked to these events, Jesus said, "The Son of man shall send forth his angels, and they shall gather out of his kingdom all things that offend, and them which do iniquity; and shall cast them into a furnace of fire: there shall be wailing and gnashing of teeth" (Matthew 13:41-42).

Earlier in this same chapter, Jesus related a significant little story commonly called the Parable of the Tares and Wheat (Matthew 13:24-30, 36-43). Both the tares and the wheat had been allowed to grow together until the harvest, but then the reapers were to gather them up in bundles. The tares were to be burned; the wheat gathered.

We often wonder why God permits so much sin in the world, why He withholds His right arm of judgment. Why doesn't God put an end to sin now? We can give an answer from this text where Jesus said, "Let both grow together," the evil with the good (v. 30). To angels will be delegated the ministry of separating the good from the bad, discerning even attitudes. God's judgment will be so pure that even those who are condemned will bow their knee and confess, "Thou art just."

So angels will not only accompany Christ when He returns, they will be assigned the responsibility of gathering out of His kingdom all things that offend and work iniquity, that they might be judged.

Read Matthew 13:47-50 in your Bible. Explore Jesus' parable by filling in the blanks.

The kingdom of heaven is like _____.
The net collected _____ _____ of fish.
The good fish were _____ while the bad fish were _____.
_____ will be God's agents of separation of righteous and evil persons.

day Five

Angels Join in Heaven's Worship

Angels possess the ultimate capacity to offer praise, and their music from time immemorial has been the primary vehicle of praise to our all-glorious God. John saw a massive heavenly choir of many millions who expressed their praise of the heavenly Lamb through magnificent music (Revelation 5:11-12). Unquestionably angels ascribe honor and glory to the Lamb of God. When angels stand before the throne of God, they worship and adore their Creator. I believe angel choirs will sing in eternity to the glory of God and the supreme delight of the redeemed.

We can look for that future day when angels will have finished their earthly ministry. Then they will gather with all the redeemed before the throne of God in heaven. There they will offer their praise and sing their songs. In that day the angels who veiled their faces and stood mute when Jesus hung on the cross will then ascribe glory to the Lamb whose work is finished and whose kingdom has come. The angels may also stop to listen as the redeemed children of God express their own thanksgiving for salvation. It may well be true, as Rev. Johnson Oatman, Jr. expressed in verse 3 of that wonderful hymn "Holy, Holy Is What the Angels Sing,"

> Then the angels stand and listen,
> for they cannot join that song,
> Like the sound of many waters,
> by that happy, blood-washed throng.

But the children of God will also stop to listen to the angels. The angels have their own reasons for singing, ones that differ from ours. They have given themselves to the service of God Almighty. They have had a part in bringing in the kingdom of God. They have helped the children of God in difficult circumstances. So theirs shall be a shout and a song of victory. The cause they represent has been victorious; the fight they fought is finished; the enemy they met has been conquered; their wicked

Week of DECEMBER 26

companion angels who fell shall vex them no more. The angels sing a different song, but they sing—my, how they sing! And I believe that angels and those of us who have been redeemed will compete with each other for the endless ages of eternity to see who can best ascribe glory and praise to our wonderful God!

How do you understand Dr. Graham's statement that angels and the redeemed "will compete with each other for the endless ages of eternity to see who can best ascribe glory and praise to . . . God"?

_____

Do you know—beyond doubt—that some day you will join the angels in heaven in singing praises to God? If not, make your commitment to Christ today. Without Christ you are separated from God and without hope of eternal life. You need to have your sins forgiven, and you need to be renewed and cleansed by the power of God. And this can happen, if you will give your life to Christ and trust Him as your personal Lord and Savior. Christ came to take away your sins by His death on the cross. You deserved to die—but He died in your place! The Bible says, "For Christ died for sins once for all, the righteous for the unrighteous, to bring you to God" (1 Peter 3:18, NIV). Right now by a simple prayer of faith you can know that some day you will join with the angels and with millions of believers from across the ages in singing praises to God in heaven. Take that step of faith today.

What was the most interesting fact you learned about angels in this four-week study? _____

_____

What was the most encouraging truth you discovered about angels? _____

_____

If you have enjoyed these Bible studies from Dr. Billy Graham and desire to purchase your own copy of his book Angels to read and study in greater detail, visit the LifeWay Christian Store serving you. Or, you can order a copy by calling 1-800-233-1123.

Amy SUMMER

leader Guide

NOTES

To the Leader:

Contact all members and prospects this week and encourage them to make attendance at weekly Bible study a regular habit in 2005.

Before the Session

1. You probably won't have time to cover all the teaching suggestions. It would be better to focus on one or two Scripture passages and gain life-changing truths rather than information from several passages.
2. Enlist volunteers to read aloud Psalm 34:7; Psalm 91:11; Romans 8:31; and 1 John 4:4.
3. Display the poster of Hebrews 1:14.

During the Session

1. Comment on Billy Graham's statement that the passage in 2 Kings 6 where Elisha saw armies of angels surrounding the city has been a great assurance and comfort to him in his ministry. Invite volunteers to share passages they have examined during the past three group sessions or in their personal study of "Angels" that have assured and comforted them. Have them state why. Remark that angels should bring us comfort because they are God's servants who work on our behalf both now and in the future. OR, Challenge adults to predict what they think will happen in 2005. Ask which of those predictions they can be assured will actually occur. Comment that one thing believers can be assured of is that God's angels will continue to serve as His ministering spirits to believers both now and in the future.
2. Request someone read Matthew 18:10 in the margin of Day 1. Ask if participants believe Christians have their own guardian angels assigned to watch over them. Comment that even if they are not sure they have a personal guardian angel, they can be assured that angels stand ready to help them. Invite the volunteers to read Psalm 34:7 and 91:11. Ask learners to listen for how Elisha saw the promise of those verses lived out as you read 2 Kings 6:14-17. Call for responses. Ask the volunteers to read Romans 8:31 and 1 John 4:4. Lead the class to explore how those promises reflect Elisha's declaration of faith in 2 Kings 6:16.

Week of DECEMBER 26

3. Read aloud 2 Chronicles 16:9a. Encourage participants that God always has His eye on them and will send His angels to provide what they need. To explore how persons in the Bible discovered that truth, instruct half the class to read the account of Hagar in Genesis 16:1-13 and the other half of the class to read about Peter's experience in Acts 12:4-11. Allow participants to share how Hagar and Peter experienced God's loving care through the ministry of angels. Request a volunteer read the final paragraph of Day 2. Invite volunteers to share their personal experiences of how angels may have guarded or guided them.

4. Ask participants to describe a party given in someone's honor that they either attended or hosted. Ask: *What was the occasion? What was done for the guest of honor? How do you think that party compares to the homecoming reception you'll receive when you enter heaven?* Summarize Dr. Graham's teachings about the angels' roles at our deaths from the material in Day 3. Invite a volunteer to read Psalm 116:15. Ask for responses to the activity at the end of Day 3. Ask how the activity of angels at a believer's death demonstrates how precious that saint's death is to God.

5. Comment that although death does not have to be feared, it is still painful for those left behind. The world will continue to suffer until Jesus' final coming. Invite someone to read Romans 8:19-23. Comment that God sends angels to minister to us as we wait and that angels will also have a role in Christ's second coming. Read Matthew 13:24-30. Write "farmer," "enemy," "weeds," "wheat," "reapers" on the board and ask participants to state who is represented by each term. Write responses next to the appropriate word. Ask participants to check their answers by silently reading Matthew 13:37-42. Read Matthew 13:47-50 and compare that parable to the parable of the wheat and tares.

6. Request someone read aloud the poster of Hebrews 1:14. Ask what angels will do when they no longer need to minister to God's people on earth. Invite someone to read Revelation 5:11-12. Ask who will join the angels in worshiping God. Read Revelation 5:13. Ask: *What reasons will the angels have for singing to God? What reasons will you have to sing praises to God?*

7. Invite participants to state sentence prayers thanking God for sending angels to minister to believers in the past, now, and in the future.

NOTES

ABOUT THE WRITERS

masterWork:
Essential Messages from God's Servants

• Designed for developing and maturing believers who desire to go deeper into the spiritual truths of God's Word.

• Ideal for many types of Bible study groups.

• A continuing series from leading Christian authors and their key messages.

• Based on LifeWay's well-known, interactive model for daily Bible study.

• The interspersed interactive personal learning activities **in bold type** are written by the writer identified on the Study Theme unit page.

• Teaching plans follow each lesson to help facilitators guide learners through lessons.

• Published quarterly.

Charles R. Swindoll wrote the lessons for the Study Theme drawn from his book *Living on the Ragged Edge*.

Dr. Swindoll is senior pastor of Stonebriar Community Church in Frisco, Texas, and chancellor of Dallas Theological Seminary. He is the author of a number of best-selling books. His radio ministry, "Insight for Living," is heard around the world on a daily basis.

AMY SUMMERS wrote the personal learning activities and teaching plans this quarter. Amy is an experienced writer for LifeWay Bible study curriculum, a wife, a mother, and a Sunday School leader from Arden, North Carolina. She is a graduate of Baylor University and Southwestern Baptist Theological Seminary.

ABOUT THIS STUDY

On the line below, place a check to indicate where you are in your life's journey.

|⊢────┼────┼────┼────┼────⊣|

I'm longing for what might be.   **I'm satisfied with what is.**

Living on the Ragged Edge

There once lived a man who had the time, the money, and the energy to take a journey to find what truly satisfies. Not just a mind trip, but in actuality. Not across imaginary back roads of his memory by simply following the blue lines on a map, but into life itself. Because he was "free to walk" and because no one was able to restrain him, he held nothing back. Thankfully, he kept an accurate journal of his journey, which is available for all to read. The man's name was Solomon, and the journal he kept is the Book of Ecclesiastes.

I should tell you that the journey this man took left him deflated, depressed, and disillusioned. The best word is *empty* … his favorite and most often repeated description of how he felt *before* he took his journey, *while* he endured his journey, and *after* the journey was over. Nothing he saw, discovered, attempted, produced, initiated, or concluded as a result of his lengthy search resulted in lasting significance or personal satisfaction.

Time after time, Solomon mentions his horizontal, strictly human viewpoint. In virtually every major section of his journal he uses the words "under the sun" and "under heaven." Because he left God out of the picture, nothing satisfied. It never will. Satisfaction in life under the sun will never occur until there is a meaningful connection with the living Lord above the sun.

Ecclesiastes has today's world woven through the fabric of every page. Change the names, the geography, the year, the culture, and you've got today's scene portrayed in living color. All around us are people who are buying into this empty, horizontal, who-needs-God perspective.

The good life—the one that truly satisfies—exists only when we stop wanting a better one. It is the condition of savoring what *is* rather than longing for what *might* be. Satisfaction comes when we step off the escalator of desire and say, "This is enough. What I have will do. What I make of it is up to me and my vital union with the living Lord."

Chuck Swindoll

Charles SWINDOLL

Chasing the Wind

day One

Telling the Truth About Existence

Many years ago there lived a king who decided he would write in a journal what he had discovered about life. His father, David, had left a rather large estate in his care. His father had fought the battles and now the son, Solomon, enjoyed peace—40 years of it. Imagine! He ruled four decades over a nation free of war.

Instead of money being poured into the war machine, peacetime money was available and Solomon used it to finance his pursuits to discover life. One day, after the pursuit was over and done, he sat down and wrote in his journal the truth about all he had discovered. There's not one lie in his book. I should warn you, however, it is not your basic *Here's How to Be Rich and Famous* volume. But it is trustworthy information all the world needs to read.

The king's journal has one basic premise, and he doesn't make us wait until the end of the book to read it. He says it right at the beginning.

> Vanity of vanities ...
> Vanity of vanities!
> All is vanity (Eccl. 1:2).

Read Ecclesiastes 1:2 in the margin. What is your initial response to Solomon's conclusion about life?

- ❏ **What a spoiled ungrateful brat!**
- ❏ **I completely identify.**
- ❏ **Is that really in the Bible?**
- ❏ **Is the entire study going to be this depressing?**

In Hebrew literature, when the same word is repeated even once, it is for the purpose of emphasis. It is like our exclamation point. It is as though Solomon wants to declare the superlative, "Super vain! Completely empty! Nothing to it!"

Week of JANUARY 2

Life appears to have substance, yet when you dig into it, there's nothing there. It holds out hope that it is a bright, warm dream; but when you go for it, you stumble into a cold, dark nightmare. Remember this counsel—It won't satisfy. It won't work.

Read Ecclesiastes 1:3 in the margin. How would you paraphrase Solomon's question?

_____

_____

"What advantage does man have in all his work … which he does under the sun?" (Eccl. 1:3).

The key word is *advantage*, which comes from the original Hebrew word meaning "that which is left over when the transaction is complete." We would say, "When it is all said and done, when you turn the light out at the end of life, when you finally close the door to your business and retire, when you walk away from the fresh grave of someone you loved, when it's 'curtains,' the final advantage is reduced to zero satisfaction."

Are you willing to believe that? Will you accept that, not as some other man's journal, but as the truth concerning your life? We who worship our work and play at our worship have gotten things fouled up. The journal writer tells us before we even begin that it's "nothingness under the sun."

"We who worship our work and play at our worship have gotten things fouled up."
— Chuck Swindoll

Take an honest look at your labor. Your financial savings decrease in value, rather than increase. You toil for a raise and the guy next to you gets the promotion. Promises for relief from the government fail. Your ship didn't come in … it sank! There's nothing left. There's no advantage.

Are you getting the depressed picture? Are you getting weary of the same old line? Good! That's exactly what the writer wanted. The sparkling jewel of hope (which he waits a long time to display) needs a somber, black backdrop of utter futility.

Circle the word(s) that best describe your response to today's study. Write the reason for your response in the margin.

Depressed   **Intrigued**   **Confused**   **Hopeful**

day Two

Examples of Futility

"A generation goes and a generation comes, but the earth remains forever" (1:4). There's futility even in the cycle. There is a group of people born this day and another group of people who will die this same day. There will be beautiful and winsome people who will die. Tough and determined people will die. Gifted, talented, and entertaining people will die. People who make us laugh, who make us think, who make us gain courage to go on will die. And some of those bright, beautiful, fun-loving, capable people will die just as empty as those who grieve at their funerals. The cycle is terribly futile.

When God arranged the solar system and flung it into space, He put purpose and meaning on the earth.

> "The sun rises and the sun sets; and hastening to its place it rises there again. Blowing toward the south, then turning toward the north, the wind continues swirling along; and on its circular courses the wind returns. All the rivers flow into the sea, yet the sea is not full" (Eccl. 1:5-7).

Read Romans 8:20 in your Bible. What happened to that original creation?

_____

_____

Consider the illustrations in Ecclesiastes 1:5-7 in the margin. What happens to the sun each day?

_____

What happens to the wind?

_____

Do you ever feel your life is as monotonous as the swirling wind or the rolling river? ❑ Yes ❑ No

Have you ever felt your life is on a boring cycle like the sun? ❑ Yes ❑ No

Week of JANUARY 2

If your purpose in life is under the sun, it's running around in circles. I think Solomon wrote verse 8 with a deep, long sigh. "All things are wearisome; man is not able to tell it."

As little children, we were told to keep looking and keep discovering. There is beauty to be found, there's wonder out there. As we get older, we get more sophisticated and start wanting telescopes and microscopes so we can look into the depths of our natural world. Yet we cannot seem to get telescopes large enough or microscopes with lenses thick enough. Our curiosity is aroused but frustrated.

What we find is not satisfaction, but another question mark. So we pursue another degree to answer that question mark, and when we get that question mark removed, there's another degree we've got to have, and still more questions fail to be answered because another dimension opens up to us, another world of endlessness. We become jaded in our sophistication or disillusioned in our futility. It is maddening! So? So we decide to become philosophers—people who talk about stuff they don't understand, but make it sound like it's everyone else's fault!

The ear isn't satisfied with the hearing. Is this new? No way. Look at verse 9: "That which has been is that which will be, and that which has been done is that which will be. So, there is nothing new under the sun."

Nothing is new out there. And if you find something that is—something you didn't know before—it still won't satisfy. Solomon in effect even says, "I'd like to forget it."

"There is no remembrance of earlier things; and also of the later things which will occur" (1:11). Have you ever felt like that at the end of the day? "I'd like to forget this day." How about at the end of a pursuit of some academic achievement? "I'd like to forget that school. All that stuff that I studied and all those hours I spent and all that work I put in, I'd just like to forget it."

Were you hoping for more optimistic reading material today? What is your response to today's study?

- ❏ **Are we going somewhere with this?**
- ❏ **I had no idea others felt this way too.**
- ❏ **I feel uncomfortable reading such dismal stuff; aren't we supposed to be joyful?**
- ❏ **Other:** _____

Charles SWINDOLL

day Three

The Searcher and His Pursuits

In Ecclesiastes 1:12, Solomon suddenly introduces himself to us. He says: "I, the Preacher, have been king over Israel in Jerusalem." Then in his next statement we see he has set his sights and is ready to push forward on his journey.

Read Ecclesiastes 1:13 in your Bible. What was Solomon's goal?

_____

Do you know someone who has a goal similar to Solomon's? Write their initials here. _____

After just a brief introduction to Ecclesiastes, what would you say to this person?

_____

_____

The words *seek* and *explore* describe Solomon's mission. In Hebrew, the word translated seek means "to investigate the roots of a matter." It's what you would do as a doctoral candidate writing your dissertation.

Solomon decided to pursue the origin of these things. He went after each subject, every objective, to find out all he could about them, how they got started, and the final results. His research was thorough.

He also *explored*. This second term means "to examine all sides." In other words, Solomon is saying, "Not only did I seek to study the gardens and the lakes and rivers and reservoirs and streams, I did experiments with them. I pursued those things to the point of getting involved."

This is the journal of a man who stopped at nothing when he sought to explore, by human wisdom, all things under the heavens. There was no limit. Full investigation!

Read Ecclesiastes 1:13 again. In the final analysis, what was Solomon's opinion?

_____

What grievous task has God given people?

_____

Week of JANUARY 2

In verse 14 Solomon says that life under the sun is "striving after wind." Actually, the words mean "chasing the wind." He says it again only a few lines later—it is "striving after wind." And he says it more strongly than ever by the end of this journal entry: "Because in much wisdom there is much grief, and increasing knowledge results in increasing pain" (1:18).

I think if teenagers were reading that they would be tempted to write in the margin of the king's journal: "Homework. What's the use?"

"I set my mind to know wisdom and to know madness and folly; I realized that this also is striving after wind" (1:17). Here the writer is saying, "I've been there."

If you want to save yourself all the consequences of wrongdoing, just listen to Solomon. In fact, we would be foolish not to listen to the man who's been there. He's even thoughtful enough to say, "I'm anxious to tell you what I experienced. ... If your life is being lived strictly on the horizontal plane ... it won't bring you lasting happiness!" That's Solomon's advice. He's been there. Let's listen. Let's learn.

The answer isn't just studying more. The only way to find satisfaction and relief from boredom is through a relationship with the living God.

Solomon writes: "I said to myself, 'Behold, I have magnified and increased wisdom more than all who were over Jerusalem before me; and my mind has observed a wealth of wisdom and knowledge.' And I set my mind to know wisdom and to know madness and folly; I realized that this also is striving after wind" (1:16-17).

He's saying, "I stopped at nothing. I have pored over it. I have been there. I gave it my best shot! I set my mind to know wisdom, madness, folly. I finally realized I was merely chasing the wind."

> "The answer isn't just studying more. The only way to find satisfaction and relief from boredom is through a relationship with the living God."
> — Chuck Swindoll

PRACTICAL RAMIFICATIONS

A couple of ideas emerge from between the lines of Solomon's journal. First, if there is nothing under the sun, our only hope must be—*beyond* it. As a minister I often find myself in a position of communicating this information to others. Most folks have their heads so firmly riveted to the here and now that they virtually ignore any other dimension in life. It's not that they consciously intend to block God out of their lives, it's just that they seldom mentally catapult themselves "above the sun." But it is there that hope shines eternal.

Second, if a man who had everything, investigated everything visible, then the one thing needed must be invisible. The only way you will find satisfaction is in believing the invisible. It's in trusting the inaudible. His name is Jesus Christ. He wants to rule your life.

Where have you placed your hope? (circle)

Under the sun   **Above the sun**

Where have you placed your trust?

The visible and audible   The invisible and inaudible

day Four

An Open Invitation

In the first chapter of his journal, we have seen that Solomon tried educational stimulation and a measure of scientific exploration, and both left him empty. Surely there's more in life than *this*! So he decided to pursue another course, to scratch some itches that had been there all his life, deep down in the eros zone.

"I said to myself, 'Come now, I will test you with pleasure. So enjoy yourself.' And behold, it too was futility" (Eccl. 2:1).

According to Ecclesiastes 2:1, whom did Solomon consult about his decision to pursue pleasure as the source of satisfaction? (circle)

God   Wise Advisors   History   Himself

I thought it interesting that Solomon began this new course in his journey by talking to himself. Rather than seeking the counsel of another wiser or more experienced than he, he plunged in with both feet.

Nor did he check into the historical record of how his father, David, endured the consequences of sensuality. He didn't even look up to God in prayer and ask for divine counsel. He talked to himself.

He didn't beat around the bush when it came time to express his evaluation of it, did he? It was just another empty experience!

Week of JANUARY 2

Solomon will save us years of heartache if we will heed what he says. Not some present-day, wild-eyed, prophet of doom, but the wisest and richest man who ever lived is telling us the truth about all the things that appeal to our erotic desires. Common sense says we'd be wise to listen.

Fun 'n' Games

Now he's off on another tangent! Solomon decides to laugh his way through life: "Laughter, I'll try that! Bring on the fun 'n' games—let's live it up! After all, it feels good to laugh and have a great time in life. Surely, that's going to bring me the satisfaction I long for. Maybe *that* holds the secret." But it didn't. His admission is as honest as it is blunt: "I said of laughter, 'It is madness,' and of pleasure, 'What does it accomplish?'" (2:2).

The man is not attacking a healthy and necessary sense of humor or periodic times of enjoyable, God-honoring pleasure. The point is: There is no lasting satisfaction if your only reason for living is to make people smile, to leave them laughing.

Do you agree with the previous statement?
❏ Yes ❏ No Explain.

_____

I can hear him now, "Well, if it isn't laughter, if it's not amusement, maybe there's something in the world of liquid spirits. Perhaps the satisfaction I'm looking for is in a bottle." "I explored with my mind how to stimulate my body with wine while my mind was guiding me wisely, and how to take hold of folly" (2:3).

Solomon is not saying, as one might say in a fit of anger or exasperation, "I think I'll go out and get bombed." No, it's like he's saying, "Maybe there is more than I realized to this fantastic world of the spirits—the kind they bottle. I think I'll try that." But, again, it fails to satisfy.

Which of the following areas have you pursued in your quest for satisfaction? Circle all that apply.

Education	**Science**	**Pleasure**
Laughter	**Alcohol**	**Drugs**

Did they satisfy? ❏ Yes ❏ No

> "Solomon will save us months, even years of heartache if we will heed what he says … Common sense says we'd be wise to listen."
> — Chuck Swindoll

Charles SWINDOLL

day Five

Chasing the Dream

> "I enlarged my works: I built homes for myself, I planted vineyards for myself; I made gardens and parks for myself, and I planted in them all kinds of fruit trees; I made ponds of water for myself from which to irrigate a forest of growing trees. I bought male and female slaves, and I had homeborn slaves. Also I possessed flocks and herds larger than all who preceded me in Jerusalem. Also, I collected for myself silver and gold, and the treasure of kings and provinces. I provided for myself male and female singers and the pleasures of men—many concubines. Then I became great and increased more than all who preceded me in Jerusalem. My wisdom also stood by me. And all that my eyes desired I did not refuse them. I did not withhold my heart from any pleasure, for my heart was pleased because of all my labor and this was my reward for all my labor" (Eccl. 2:4-10).

Terribly disillusioned that several of his fantasies have been nothing more than bad dreams, Solomon decides to roll up his sleeves and really go to work. Maybe that is the answer—not projects that the nation requires of him, but personal projects. He refers to "I" and "my" many times in this section of his journal. It's intensely personal. Read it in the margin.

As you read the remainder of this section, underline statements that reflect Solomon's level of satisfaction resulting from his personal pursuits.

He tried architecture. He decided he would design beautiful structures. Indeed he did! When that didn't satisfy, he decided to take on horticulture and agriculture. He planted vineyards, lovely gardens, and sprawling parks. He needed ponds of water to keep the place green, so he dug reservoirs and had irrigation canals carved along the terrain. This man stopped at nothing, yet he remained lonely, always restless, never fulfilled.

Then Solomon decided what he needed could be provided by other people only, and so he bought them, too. "I bought male and female slaves, and I had homeborn slaves." He filled the place with slaves. He had them reproduce, and they had their own harems. Still he wasn't satisfied.

"I possessed flocks and herds larger than all who preceded me in Jerusalem" (2:7). He would have more than anyone else. He then moved into collecting precious gems and articles of silver and gold, "the treasure of kings and provinces." He even brought in male and female singers.

He wrote over a thousand songs and perhaps he put some of his compositions in front of the singers and they sight-read his work. Here he was, surrounded by his own forest and personally designed gardens and vineyards and trees. His own music filled the chambers of his houses and echoed through the forest, yet he *still* failed to find inner peace.

Next Solomon chose to turn to "the pleasures of men—many concubines." The attitude of "if it feels good, do it" has done a number on us.

Week of JANUARY 2

We live in the dream, on the brink of some great hope that's just beyond the chasm. "If I could just earn that amount, I could buy that dream and *that* thing would do it." Solomon says, "Don't go to the trouble!"

The problem is that you've got to live with yourself. And, unless you are most unusual, in the process of time you lose those things that are the most important to you—those things that make life worth living.

"All that my eyes desired I did not refuse them. I did not withhold my heart from any pleasure, for my heart was pleased because of all my labor and this was my reward for all my labor" (2:10). What was his reward? Feeling good. It sounds so appealing, so tantalizing. Yet, in reality, when the fun 'n' games are over, it's the pits. I know. It's my job to work with those folks after the party is over. The pleasure came, but it didn't last.

Review the statements you underlined about Solomon and star the ones that describe you.

Are you willing to stay with this study to the end to discover Solomon's final conclusion about the source of satisfaction? ❑ Yes ❑ No ❑ I'm not sure

TIME TO FACE THE TRUTH

Solomon's wrap-up counsel deserves prime-time exposure.

"I considered all my activities which my hands had done and the labor which I had exerted, and behold all vanity and striving after wind and there was no profit under the sun" (2:11). A few lines later Solomon adds: "There is nothing better for a man than to eat and drink and tell himself that his labor is good" (2:24).

Solomon says it straight. He's been there, he ought to know. I'd paraphrase his comments in three truthful sentences.

1. *Sensual pleasures hold out promises that lack staying power.* It does feel good at first, but it doesn't have staying power, so it takes more of the same. It's never enough.

2. *Sensual pleasures offer to open our eyes, but in reality they blind us.* That world blinds you of all the things that are important and real.

3. *Sensual pleasures disillusion us, making us cover-up artists.* We refuse to tell ourselves and others the truth about our emptiness. "If it feels good, do it" has a flip side which is neither attractive nor satisfying."

In the space below, write a prayer of repentance and/or commitment to look to God for satisfaction rather than sensual pleasures.

leader Guide

NOTES

To the Leader:

In these teaching plans you will be given two create interest options for beginning the session. The first option is geared more toward those classes that prefer a discussion format. The second option will give you ideas for a more interactive icebreaker. Choose, adapt, intertwine, or recreate one or both of those options until you have a create interest step that will lead the participants in your class to desire to explore what God's Word has to say to them through the study.

Before the Session

1. Prayerfully choose the teaching steps that will help your class explore the material in Week 1.
2. Collect objects (or obtain pictures) that have little substance such as: cotton candy, rice cake, Styrofoam, a picture of fog or mist, an unopened bag of potato chips.
3. Obtain several Bible translations of Ecclesiastes 1:2.

During the Session

1. Ask participants if they have kept a journal. Ask if they would be willing for their journals to be published and why or why not. Briefly introduce Ecclesiastes, using the introductory material on page 55. Ask: *What can we gain from reading Solomon's journal of his quest for satisfaction?* OR Pass around the objects you collected. Ask what they all have in common. Invite volunteers to read Ecclesiastes 1:2 from several Bible translations. Ask how Solomon's view of life is similar to the objects. Inquire: *What can we possibly gain from a book of the Bible that begins by stating everything is empty and meaningless?*

2. Invite someone to read Ecclesiastes 1:3. Ask adults to paraphrase Solomon's question. Inquire: *Is that a legitimate question or just the griping of a burned-out person? Why?* According to Dr. Swindoll's comment in the margin on page 57, what is the main reason our work is often pointless? Request adults share their responses to the final activity of Day 1.

3. Invite a volunteer to read Ecclesiastes 1:5-11. Ask how Solomon's description of creation reflects his observation of life in Ecclesiastes 1:2. Lead the class to give present-day examples of the truth that humanity's eyes and ears are never satisfied. Ask: *Why do people tend to look for something new rather than rejoice in the world's "sameness"?* What phrase did Solomon use in verse 9 that gives a clue he will never find satisfaction where he is looking? [under the sun] Draw a sun at the top of the board or writing surface. Request a volunteer read

Week of JANUARY 2

Romans 8:20. Ask why this earth cannot provide satisfaction. Request someone read the last sentence of Day 1. Lead a discussion on how Dr. Swindoll painted the black backdrop in Days 1 and 2. Instruct adults to listen for the glimmer of hope as you read Romans 8:20-21. Encourage adults to keep that glimmer of hope in mind as the study continues to lead them down the dark path of Solomon's journey.

4. Invite someone to read Ecclesiastes 1:12-18. Ask adults to state where Solomon looked first to find satisfaction. Write responses on the board. Discuss the margin activity and the second activity in Day 3 (p. 60). Allow volunteers to share how they have observed the truth declared in Ecclesiastes 1:18. Read Philippians 4:4. Ask how learners reconcile Solomon's gloomy statements about life with the command in Philippians 4:4. To continue exploring that question, invite someone to read the quotation in the margin on page 61. Ask how that principle applies to Bible study as well. Comment: The problem isn't with education and exploration, the problem is the focus of those activities. Ask rhetorically: *Can wisdom and education under the sun ever bring satisfaction?* Cross out the responses recorded earlier on the board.

5. Read Ecclesiastes 2:1 and ask adults to identify the second source of satisfaction Solomon explored. Write "pleasure" on the board. Discuss the first question in Day 4. Ask: *Why don't most people consult others before pursuing physical pleasures?* Request a volunteer read the quotation in the margin of Day 4. Ask: *What is Solomon saying?* Cross out "pleasure" on the board. Invite someone to read Ecclesiastes 2:2-3. Instruct the class to identify the next things Solomon looked to for satisfaction. Write responses on the board and immediately cross them out. Ask why those pursuits do not satisfy.

6. Instruct adults to circle the words "I" and "my" as they silently read Ecclesiastes 2:4-10 in Day 5. Ask: *What was the problem with Solomon's pursuit of satisfaction?* Write "Self-gratification" on the board. Ask adults to describe how Solomon felt about all his attempts at personal satisfaction. Ask someone to read Ecclesiastes 2:11. Cross out "Self-gratification." Ask: *Why do pursuits that are "all about me" always fail to satisfy?*

7. Ask: *If you could meet with Solomon at this point in his journey, where would you tell him to seek satisfaction?* Read Psalm 90:14 as a closing prayer.

NOTES

More Miles of Bad Road

day One

The Search Continues

Since Solomon was still in possession of his mental faculties, he decided to put his mind to work. If all the sensual delights and practical projects wouldn't produce lasting happiness, maybe a change in direction would.

"So I turned" (Eccl. 2:12). The new direction led him into three comparisons. He would compare wisdom with foolishness (2:13-17), the immediate with the ultimate (2:18-21), and daily work with evening relief (2:22-23). These things didn't satisfy any more than his previous pursuits.

WISDOM COMPARED TO FOOLISHNESS

Solomon's goal was to determine whether he would adopt a lifestyle marked by wisdom or by folly. (See 2:12-16.)

> As you read Ecclesiastes 2:12-16 in the margin, follow these instructions:
> 1. Write a *W* next to descriptions of a wise person.
> 2. Write an *F* next to descriptions of a foolish person.
> 3. Circle statements that describe the fate experienced by the wise and foolish.

As he states it, "A wise person walks through life with eyes wide open, lots of clear-thinking vision. But the fool operates as if in a dark room, not knowing what's up next. He gropes and wanders all around. But in the final analysis, both wise and foolish are impacted by the same fate—death."

"There is no lasting remembrance of the wise man as [is true] with the fool, inasmuch as in the coming days all will be forgotten" (2:16). How hard we try to keep that from happening! We build our tombstones out of granite. We etch the names into solid stone and hope time and weather won't wear the words away. These graves represent our loved ones and we

---

"I turned to consider wisdom, madness and folly, for what will the man do who will come after the king except what has already been done? And I saw that wisdom excels folly as light excels darkness. The wise man's eyes are in his head, but the fool walks in darkness. And yet I know that one fate befalls them both. Then I said to myself, 'As is the fate of the fool, it will also befall me. Why then have I been extremely wise?' So I said to myself, 'This too is vanity.' For there is no lasting remembrance of the wise man as with the fool, inasmuch as in the coming days all will be forgotten. And how the wise man and the fool alike die!"
(Eccl. 2:12-16).

Week of JANUARY 9

never want them forgotten. But all tombstones eventually do wear down and the names grow faint. Memories do finally fade.

"So I hated life, for the work which had been done under the sun was grievous to me; because everything is futility and striving after wind" (2:17). Have you ever felt like that? The journey continues, but the scenery doesn't change. Maybe Solomon's perspective could be enhanced if he would consider the possibility of building an enterprise from scratch, then leaving his fortune to his children. Maybe that will give him satisfaction.

THE IMMEDIATE COMPARED TO THE ULTIMATE

If I read Solomon's words correctly in 2:18-21, he decides to address not only death, but also the ultimate legacy of one who has been successful. One day all the estate will fall into the hands of the person's sons and daughters. Is that going to work?

> **Read Ecclesiastes 2:18-21 in the margin. Is Solomon's plan going to bring meaning to his life's work?**
> ❑ Yes   ❑ No   ❑ Not sure   Why?
> _____

"I hated all the fruit of my labor for which I had labored under the sun, for I must leave it to the man who will come after me. And who knows whether he will be a wise man or a fool? Yet he will have control over all the fruit of my labor for which I have labored by acting wisely under the sun. This too is vanity. Therefore I completely despaired of all the fruit of my labor for which I had labored under the sun. When there is a man who has labored with wisdom, knowledge and skill, then he gives legacy to one who has not labored with them. This too is vanity and a great evil" (Eccl. 2:18-21).

I don't care how capable, how competent, how perfectly suited your children may be to continue your dream, you were the original dreamer, the tough-minded pioneer. And no matter how closely you've had your children work alongside you, there's something you've got that they lack.

There is a price to be paid for building an empire, isn't there? The empire must be turned over to the very ones you haven't prepared for such requirements and assignments (2:20-21).

DAILY WORK COMPARED TO EVENING RELIEF

So Solomon thinks maybe the answer is taking time off in the evening to prepare his family to handle the empire, maybe that will satisfy. Look at his remarks about this in verses 22-23.

How many entrepreneurs do you know who really kick back in the evening? Can you honestly name a half dozen really success-driven people who leave all their work at the office?

Perhaps Solomon's mind was on his son, Rehoboam. After four decades of peace, Solomon handed over this kingdom to his son.

"What does a man get in all his labor and in his striving with which he labors under the sun? Because all his days his task is painful and grievous; even at night his mind does not rest. This too is vanity" (Eccl. 2:22-23).

Rehoboam could choose to seek counsel from the seasoned men of God who would warn him, or listen to the young, self-serving upstarts who cared nothing about God. He chose the latter.

Perhaps Solomon foresaw tragedy in the life of his unprepared, impulsive son and was saying, "Not even when I spend an evening at rest do I see the possibility of hope in my boy."

**Do Solomon's concerns listed below concern you as well? Circle Yes or No and briefly explain why.
My fate will be no different than everyone else's.**

Yes No _____
Who can I trust to continue my legacy and hard work?

Yes No _____
When can I get true rest and peace? Yes   No

_____

day Two

A Flash of Insight

Solomon gets a rare flash of insight that grabs his attention. And it comes, ironically, on the heels of this bleak series of frustrating scenes. "There is nothing in a man to eat and drink and tell himself that his labor is good" (2:24).

Here is his first flash of insight: *There is nothing inherent in humanity that makes it possible for us to extract enjoyment and purpose from the things we do.* Solomon said, 'There is nothing within you (or your children) that will automatically give happiness, keep peace, or bring joy." Riches will not result in the satisfied life. Happiness cannot be purchased.

The next line in Solomon's journal offers a second flash of insight: *Enjoyment is God's personal gift.*

"Who can eat and who can have enjoyment without Him?" (2:25). Unless God is in the middle of it, lasting enjoyment is impossible. Is there

Week of JANUARY 9

any place better to be than with a group of Christians who get together and enjoy fellowship?

If you really want to have fun, you need only one ingredient in your midst; you need a relationship with the living God. As God's people, we're the ones who ought to be having the time of our lives!

Now comes Solomon's third flash of insight: *Those who are right with God derive the benefit of everyone's labor.* The world thinks it's building its fortune for itself, yet, ultimately, the Christian benefits from most of it. "To a person who is good in His sight He has given wisdom and knowledge and joy, while to the sinner He has given the task of gathering and collecting so that he may give to one who is good in God's sight. This too is vanity and striving after wind" (2:26).

If you don't have Jesus Christ in the nucleus of your plans, you are facing endless miles of bad road. And you're left with years of sleepless nights and nothing to show for it when they put you in the box.

Bad roads and futile dead-end streets aren't limited to non-Christians. The difference comes in being able to persevere in spite of the difficulty. Without Christ, there is no way through.

In the margin write the three insights Solomon recorded in Ecclesiastes 2:24-26. Draw a star next to the insights you have personally observed. Check those insights you need to ponder more for greater understanding.

OUR GIFT OF TIME

Let's pretend your banker told you that an anonymous donor who loves you very much has decided to deposit 86,400 pennies into your account each morning, 7 days a week, 52 weeks a year. He adds, "But you must spend all the money *that same day*. No balance will be carried over to the next day." You start figuring: that's almost $315,000 a year *if* you're diligent to spend it all each day.

Every morning Someone who loves you very much deposits into your bank of time 86,400 seconds—24 hours. The same stipulation applies. Nothing is carried over to the next day.

We all have the same amount of time. Whether we are penniless or rich, young or old, single or married, employed or without a job—we have exactly the same amount of time.

Solomon's Insights

1. _____
   _____
   _____
2. _____
   _____
   _____
3. _____
   _____
   _____

Rank the amount of time you feel you have by placing an X on the line below.

|———————|———————|———————|———————|

**Time passes
too slowly.**   **My time is
about right.**   **I never have
enough time.**

What Is Time?
The best definition I have read is "a stretch of duration in which things happen." Whether we are awake or asleep, conscious or unconscious, serving it well or wasting it, time is a duration, a measurable period, in which things happen.

Why Is Time So Important?
Time is completely irretrievable. You can never repeat it or relive it. It travels alongside us every day, yet it has eternity wrapped up in it.

When Will Time End?
Will time be here forever or will it come to an end? Since man invented the clock, obviously that device will not be with us throughout eternity. The planets that were arranged in space by almighty God continue to be the most perfect chronometer, but when those planets stop, time stops. So time is temporary. And that means we need to invest it wisely and find ways to enjoy it while it is ours to claim.

> "There is nothing better for a man than to eat and drink and tell himself that his labor is good. This also I have seen, that it is from the hand of God. For who can eat and who can have enjoyment without Him?" (Eccl. 2:24–25).

I think this dimension of life caused Solomon to pull over from his journey to write a practical analysis of time in his journal. He seems to have been prompted to do that toward the end of the chapter we just concluded. Remember his closing comment? Read it again in the margin.

So far in Solomon's journey he has sought ways to enjoy his time while it lasted. Where did he seek that enjoyment? U_____ the S_____ (see 2:11). Did he find it? ❏ Yes ❏ No

In Ecclesiastes 2:24-25 Solomon finally declared there is enjoyment in this life. What is the source of that enjoyment? The H_____ of G_____.

Week of JANUARY 9

What is from the hand of God? The ability to work, the ability to eat, the ability to drink, the ability to tell one's self that life is good—all of it comes from the hand of God. And without Him, none of these things can be enjoyed. Apart from Him and the perspective that He alone can give, what is there to laugh about? Or who is there to laugh with? You can't even have enjoyment or an appetite without God.

day Three

Life: Measured by Events (Part 1)

After pondering the whole idea of not being able to enjoy life apart from God, the writer breaks life down into measurable chunks that he calls "events." "There is an appointed time for everything. And there is a time for every event under heaven" (3:1).

In Ecclesiastes 3:1-8, Solomon listed the events of life with a series of opposites. Keep your Bible open throughout today's study and fill in the blanks to complete each set of opposites.

1. *A time to give birth, and a time to* _____. You cannot hasten either. You haven't the control over those things. Those are given to you by God; you are the recipient of birth and you are the recipient of death.

Depressed people have a tendency to ask: Why was I born? Why can't I die? It seems as though when life boils itself down to the basics, we go back to birth and death.

2. *A time to* _____, *and a time to uproot what is planted*. Most of us have never worked the fields or harvested crops. But we're smart enough to know that there is a time for planting and a time for uprooting. You don't plant when it's harvest time. And when the fruit is ripe, you must see that it's picked promptly. Timing is everything when it comes to the field.

This is also true on a personal level. God has a way of uprooting us and planting us, and He does it in His time.

**Are you feeling uprooted OR planted at this point in your life? Circle your answer.
How does the truth that God has appointed this time of your life help you accept it gratefully?**

_____

3. *A time to _____, and a time to heal.* We don't like this part. Life seems somewhere strangely fixed between a battlefield and a first-aid station, between murder and medicine.

There is the Mafia in one part of our world and a Mother Teresa type figure in another. Sometimes they appear in adjacent columns in our newspaper, and we are forced to deal with those opposites, killing and healing, at the same point in time.

What needs to be torn down in your life?

_____

_____

What needs to be built up?

_____

_____

4. *A time to tear down, and a time to _____ _____.* A perfect illustration is urban renewal. Demolition crews are followed by construction crews. We see it in the restoration of old homes. We see it in the familiar scenes of life. There is a tearing-down time, and there is a building-up time.

5. *A time to _____, and a time to laugh.* Are you weeping these days? Low tides are hard times. And you long for times to laugh because they're much more enjoyable. Though I am convinced laughter does not teach us as much as tears, I love to laugh. I desire to cultivate a good sense of humor. I am not too concerned that my family remember the rules and regulations that came from my lips, but I hope they never forget the sound of my laughter. I hope it is absorbed in the walls of my home.

6. *A time to mourn, and a time to _____.* As a pastor I've seen families in a dark funeral parlor leaning hard on one another, enduring the loss of a family member. I've also seen children in fractured families mourn the divorce of parents. Sometimes I think a death would have been less painful. What mourning!

Then I've seen that same family, less than a year later, dance at the reception of a daughter who got married. How quickly the scene of mourning can change to dancing.

Read back through the list of six opposites and circle the events you are presently experiencing. In the margin, write a prayer of gratitude to God for perfectly appointing the times of your life.

Week of JANUARY 9

day Four

Life: Measured by Events (Part 2)

As you continue your study of Ecclesiastes 3:2-8, again fill in the blanks to complete each set of opposites.

7. *A time to throw stones, and a time to* _____ *stones.*
8. *A time to* _____, *and a time to shun embracing.*

I link the throwing of stones with the shunning of embraces and the gathering of stones with the times to embrace. And I take this to mean times of affirmation pushed up next to times of confrontation.

There are occasions when we need the embrace of a friend encouraging us not to quit, reminding us that life will go on. And then there are times when that same person may confront us with the hard truth, "I think what you are doing is wrong." For a life to stay balanced, both affirmation and accountability are needed.

Verse 6 introduces an interesting opposite:

9. *A time to* _____, *and a time to give up as lost.* Rescue squads continually face this dilemma. They search and search through days and nights, sometimes the search wears on for weeks. A similar human drama occurred not far from where I live. Little three-year-old Laura Bradbury somehow was separated from her parents at Joshua Tree National Monument. The search continued for 20 anguishing days before authorities decided the search should be stopped. In the opinion of the experts, it was time to "give up as lost."

10. *A time to keep, and a time to* _____ _____.
I think of my closet when I read that line, don't you? There's a time to clean out the garage and get rid of that stuff. There's a time to rid yourself of excess baggage and get a fresh start on life. And there's a time to keep. Some things you never throw away. Some things you would rather die than part with.

11. *A time to tear apart, and a time to sew* _____. That seems to go with the previous phrase. The next one—how I wish I knew this ahead of time!

Charles SWINDOLL

12. *A time to be _____, and a time to speak.* Don't you wish someone invisible could stay near you to say, "Psst, speak up," when you should or, "Psst, be quiet; don't talk"? More often than not we're wise to say less. However, there are times when we need to stand and speak, even when others might think we look foolish. When we can make a contribution, we should do so. We are responsible to declare our convictions, to be true to our character, and to be true to our heritage.

**Do you more often have a problem with being silent OR speaking up? Circle your answer.
Ask God to help you recognize and obey the right time to do both.**

____ Your teenager has been arrested after another wild night with the wrong crowd.

____ Your friend is contemplating placing his mother in an assisted living center.

____ Your brother is working 80 hours a week and spending little time with his family.

____ You are working 80 hours a week and spending little time with your family.

____ Friends from your Sunday School class are getting a divorce.

____ Colleagues from work are increasingly engaging in unethical behavior.

____ You and your spouse don't have much to talk about these days.

13. *A time to love, and a time to _____.* Here is another contrast that makes us uncomfortable. There is a time to demonstrate love, but there is also a time to hate. Acts of injustice, acts of prejudice, and inequities ought to be hated.

Finally, the ancient king mentions a contrast that applies most directly to us as a nation.

14. *A time for _____, and a time for peace.* When tyranny runs roughshod over the rights of mankind, war is necessary. We worship without the fear of infringement from law because someone has fought for our right to be heard and to speak freely, to stand and (if necessary) die for what one believes to be the truth.

Solomon adds: "And there must be a time for peace." Are you a peacemaker? Do you keep the peace? Are you aware we are to "keep the unity of the Spirit in the bond of peace"?

When you look back over this list of opposites, perhaps you begin to feel a tension that can't be overlooked. Sometimes you and I don't know which is the appropriate reaction. Other times we know which we should do, yet the timing is not right. To do the right thing at the wrong time can be almost as inappropriate as failing to do the right thing at all. Frequently, our questions leave us with further questions.

Read the list of life situations in the margin. Next to each situation, write the numbers 7 through 14 to indicate which of Solomon's opposites discussed in Day 4 either represent the tension you might feel in that situation or give you direction as to how you

Week of JANUARY 9

should respond to that scenario. Don't expect this to be easy, use this exercise to gain experience in prayerfully seeking God's perspective on the timing of events in your life.

day Five

Questions and Conclusions

Two questions seem to leap from the page of Solomon's journal when we come to the end of this list. One is stated; the other, implied.

Read Ecclesiastes 3:9. What is Solomon's first question? _____

When you look at life and you slice it down to the essentials, what's the profit? What is the gain? What is the reason?

That's not only the point of this section, that's the message of this entire journal. If it's only a horizontal trip from birth to death; if you leave God out of the scene, life will still be profitless. It's all so empty.

The second question is: *What's the purpose?* Where's life going? You may get a graduate school degree; you may earn several of them. But you still won't learn where life is going.

This chapter has endured just long enough to get most of you bored. Solomon planned it that way. It's to show you how futile and empty life is.

ALL-IMPORTANT CONCLUSIONS

What we need are some conclusions that take away the futility. Solomon provides that. He even brings the name of God into it. What a shocker for a man on a horizontal journey!

"I have seen the tasks which God has given the sons of men with which to occupy themselves. He has made everything appropriate in its time" (3:10–11). God has made everything appropriate in His time. That's such an important, never-to-be-forgotten statement! It's the first time in this skeleton of thought that the writer has given you something he can build on "*above* the heavens."

How much we fail to see when we miss God's timing! But when we see it through His eyes, the beautiful picture comes together; and as it does, we give Him praise.

I see His sovereign hand at work as He is reminding us He is still in charge. And I acknowledge my need for greater dependence. As I do that, I willingly relinquish the controls to Him. So easy to say. So hard to do.

Now for the second conclusion: "He has also set eternity in their heart, yet so that man will not find out the work which God has done from the beginning even to the end" (3:11). God has put eternity in our hearts. What in the world does that mean? The key word is *eternity*. Let's expand it to mean "curiosity about our future."

God has not only put things into perspective by having a timetable in which events run their course, He has also put within every human heart a curiosity about tomorrow—an eternal capacity that prompts me to probe, to be intrigued, to search. We will not find out about tomorrow without God; our pursuit must be of Him.

Let's put all this together. Write Solomon's two questions and conclusions in the margin. In your opinion, how do the conclusions answer the questions?

Time has begun for you and me, but it hasn't yet ended, by His grace. Are you ready for that moment when God will "blot out time and start the wheel of eternity"? If you're not absolutely sure that at the breathing of your last breath you have heaven as your destiny, you're not really ready to live. I point you to Jesus Christ who came to give men and women hope, forgiveness, and assurance, along with eternity in their hearts.

Take God's gift of eternal life while you still have time. There's a time to reject and a time to accept.

Make this your time to accept eternal life by prayerfully reading the front inside cover of this publication. Talk with your pastor or Bible Study leader about questions you have or to inform them of your decision to accept Christ.

Questions:
1. What is the
_____?
2. What is the
_____?

Conclusions:
1. God has made everything
_____ in its
_____.
2. God has set
_____
in our hearts.

Week of JANUARY 9

leader Guide

Before the Session
1. Prayerfully choose the teaching steps you feel will help your class explore and understand the material in Week 2.
2. Gather several denominations of coins and bills—one for each participant present.

During the Session
1. Announce: *It's time to begin our study.* Ask the class to state other examples of how the word *time* is used in daily dialogue. Ask why time figures so prominently in our conversations. Inquire: *Based on what you know about Solomon so far, what do you think he would say is the purpose of the time we spend engaged in our many activities?* OR Distribute the money you collected earlier to each participant. Ask: *If one cent equals one hour, how much time are you holding in your hand?* Request participants turn to a partner and discuss what they would do with the hours they are holding. Ask the class: *What is the purpose of the activities on which you're going to spend your hours?*
2. Draw a horizontal line on the board and comment there is no purpose to time if our focus in spending our time is horizontal and under the sun. Draw a vertical line through the horizontal line, forming a cross, and comment: *Time is meaningless and cannot be enjoyed unless we venture vertically beyond the sun.* Declare that Solomon had to travel many miles of bad road before he reached that conclusion.
3. Request a volunteer read Ecclesiastes 2:12-16. Ask participants to state the conclusions Solomon reached in his comparison of wisdom and foolishness. Ask: *What kind of wisdom do you think Solomon was talking about? How would you answer Solomon's question, "What's the point of being wise?" Do you think the wise and foolish suffer the same fate? Why? How is a fool's death different than a wise person's death?* Ask participants whether they have ever sold one home to move to another. Invite them to describe how they felt about someone else taking over their yard, workshop, or kitchen. Direct participants to

NOTES

To the Leader:

Prayerfully read Ecclesiastes 3:1-8 and consider how it relates to your class. Is it time for a new class to be birthed from yours? What worldly lies need to be uprooted so the truth of God's Word can be firmly planted in participants' hearts? Does your class need to mourn or laugh right now? Is it time for you to be silent and let someone else speak? Thank God that He has made your class and you as a teacher beautiful in its time.

NOTES

silently read Ecclesiastes 2:18-21 and compare their feelings about selling their home to Solomon's comments. Read Ecclesiastes 2:22-23. Ask the class to state Solomon's final conclusion of his three comparisons.

4. Ask someone to read Ecclesiastes 2:24-26. Use the first and third activities in Day 2 to generate a discussion about Solomon's insights into a truly satisfied life. Ask: *Why do you think those insights led him to ponder the issue of time?*

5. Request participants list the statements Solomon made about time in Ecclesiastes 3:2-8. Lead the class to discuss: 1) how people try to take control over all these events; 2) which of these statements are particularly meaningful or challenging to them right now and why; 3) how the truth that God has appointed each of these times in their lives helps them endure or appreciate that event more fully. Discuss the life situations listed in the margin on page 76, using the directions to the final activity in Day 4.

6. Invite a volunteer to read Ecclesiastes 3:9-11. Allow participants to share their responses to the second activity in Day 5. You may need to help the class understand the only way their time spent in activities has profit and purpose is if it leads them to seek God's eternal life and God's perspective of life here on earth.

7. Ask: *Suppose Solomon came to you and asked, "What must I do with my time so I can leave my children and nation a legacy that will last?" How would you answer?* Read Psalm 90:12 as a closing prayer.

Optional Activity—if you would like to delve deeper into the study of time, lead the class to read the following Scriptures and discuss what the Bible says is the proper use of and attitude toward time: Psalm 31:14-15; Psalm 39:4-7; Ephesians 5:15-17; Colossians 4:5.

Week of JANUARY 16

Interlude of Rare Insight

day One

Life with God

Life *without God* is the pits. That's the way God designed it. He placed within us that God-shaped vacuum that only He can fill. Until He is there, nothing satisfies. In this section of Solomon's journal we will see what God *makes*, what God *gives*, and what God *does*.

WHAT GOD MAKES

Read Ecclesiastes 3:11 in the margin and fill in the blank. When we look at life through God's eyes we discover He makes everything _____.

> "He has made everything beautiful in its time. He has also set eternity in the hearts of men; yet they cannot fathom what God has done from beginning to end" (Eccl. 3:11, NIV).

He makes everything "beautiful in its time" (NIV). This includes your loss, your failures, your brokenness, your battles, your fragmented dreams, even your terminal illness. God wouldn't say "everything" if He didn't mean "everything." He makes it beautiful in its time.

Have you personally experienced the truth that God makes everything beautiful in its time? Briefly describe your experience.

_____

"He has also set eternity in their heart"—*He makes everybody curious.* God has given us that eternal itch for tomorrow. He gives us a hunger to know what's next. God has given mankind the ability to see beyond the present. He has given us eternity in our hearts, without which "man will not find out the work which God has done from the beginning even to *the end.*"

He's *given* me that curiosity about the ending. Without that curiosity, I will never discover that there is a God.

What God Gives

> "I know that there is nothing better for them than to rejoice and to do good in one's lifetime, moreover, that every man who eats and drinks sees good in all his labor—it is the gift of God" (Eccl. 3:12-13).

Read Ecclesiastes 3:12-13 in the margin and underline four gifts God gives His people.

God gives us the ability to rejoice and enjoy life. There's nothing better for us than to rejoice. Have you ever seen a person who didn't have God truly enjoying life on a regular basis? The only one who enjoys and exudes the gift of rejoicing is the believer. God alone can give the perspective and refreshing hope needed to sustain a life of joy, regardless.

God gives us the ability to do good in our lifetime. God gives us the ability to do good whether or not others do us good in return. It doesn't come from any heart of love and compassion, because you and I don't have hearts like that. But when God, in the person of Jesus Christ, comes into a life, He gives that once-selfish individual the capacity to do good without being thanked, getting credit, or receiving applause. You find yourself motivated to do good, because God's life is at work in you.

God gives us an appetite to eat and to drink. This is the gift of appetite—the ability to enjoy our food. That appetite comes from God, as does our entire internal mechanism. It's just like a good night's sleep. You cannot buy the ability to fall asleep and rest peacefully through the night. That is a gift from God.

God gives us the ability to see good in all our labor. I call it *perspective*. Under-the-sun perspective says, "I earn what I get." Above-the-sun perspective says, "You get what you will never deserve and can never earn"—forgiveness, eternal life, grace, hope, life beyond the grave, a reason to go on, regardless.

> "I know that everything God does will remain forever; there is nothing to add to it and there is nothing to take from it, for God has so worked that men should fear Him. That which is has been already, and that which will be has already been, for God seeks what has passed by" (Eccl. 3:14-15).

What God Does

The best is saved until the last—what God *does* (3:14-15). Whatever God does is *permanent*. "It will remain forever." It'll be there tomorrow and for an eternity of tomorrows. God's work is *thorough and complete*. Nothing can be added to it (there's nothing missing when it comes) and nothing can be taken from it (it's never excessive or superfluous). It's never too

Week of JANUARY 16

little, too late, too much, or too early. And when you see the work of God, you stand in awe.

That's the third thing God does. He performs things that cultivate respect for Him. You don't glance at pictures of Mount Everest and say, "Hmm, nice hill." You don't witness the glaciers in Alaska and say, "Oh, yeah, that's a pretty nice glacier." You stand in silent awe.

God patiently repeats things until they are learned. We get weary of learning the lesson, and we run from it. Yet God repeats it and repeats it until the light comes on and we learn it. God seeks what we try to escape. God makes a permanent lesson out of what you think is a temporary and passing experience.

What permanent lessons might God be teaching you through a situation you are presently experiencing?

_____

LIFE FROM GOD

The only place we can find life from God is at the source—Jesus Christ. That's the basis of the gospel. Christ alone will give you the life of God.

Life from God is supernatural power now—not a vague force limited to a long time ago. God dispenses His supernatural power to anyone who says, "I want it." It doesn't cost a thing. All you have to do is take a gift. And the gift is the power of God, through faith in His Son.

Maybe it's time for you to pause and take care of that issue once and for all. When you do, the Force will not only be *with* you, it will be *in* you.

day two

Confessions of a Cynic

Remember the theme of the king's journal? Everything is barren, futile emptiness. The man who writes it is not sad, he's mad. The injustices in life have taken their toll. So it is with us. We can handle affliction and mistreatment so long as it passes. But if the pain persists and the hurt is not relieved, we become cynics. When we get near the edge of panic, we look

"I have seen under the sun that in the place of justice there is wickedness, and in the place of righteousness there is wickedness. I said to myself, 'God will judge both the righteous man and the wicked man,' for a time for every matter and for every deed is there. I said to myself concerning the sons of men, 'God has surely tested them in order for them to see that they are but beasts.' For the fate of the sons of men and the fate of beasts is the same. As one dies so dies the other; indeed, they all have the same breath and there is no advantage for man over beast, for all is vanity. All go to the same place. All came from the dust and all return to the dust. Who knows that the breath of man ascends upward and the breath of the beast descends downward to the earth? And I have seen that nothing is better than that man should be happy in his activities, for that is his lot. For who will bring him to see what will occur after him?" (Eccl. 3:16-22).

up and cry out against God. And if we don't have the faith to get us through such horizontal injustices, we simply die cynics.

Solomon is not near death, but he is fast approaching rank cynicism. And since his perspective is strictly horizontal, we are not surprised to find that his patience is running thin.

Read Ecclesiastes 3:16-22 in the margin. Use the chart below to compare what Solomon was looking for with what he actually found.

Solomon looked for ...	Instead he found ...
_____	_____
_____	_____
_____	_____
_____	_____

In your opinion, why would Solomon's conclusions lead to cynicism?

_____

The phrases "I have seen" and "I said to myself" underscore a basic, philosophical commitment to human perspective. You will not find Solomon on his knees, but on his feet. You will not find Solomon looking up, but looking out. You won't find Solomon quietly seeking patience in prayer, but rather shouting back at God. Driven from the human point of view, looking strictly on this earth and not into the heavens, Solomon sneers, "There is no advantage for man over beast."

THE PROBLEM THAT CREATES CYNICISM

Solomon's opening statement may give us some insight into the problem that caused him to fall into such a cynical slump (3:16). There is something amazingly relevant about this problem of wickedness winning over justice.

If life can't be comfortable, at least it can be fair! Solomon, too, felt life's injustice as he describes in the following observation: "Then I looked again at all the acts of oppression which were being done under the sun.

Week of JANUARY 16

And behold I saw the tears of the oppressed and that they had no one to comfort them; and on the side of their oppressors was power, but they had no one to comfort them" (4:1).

Can you feel the sigh in his words? There is something within humanity that longs for judicial justification.

Later the same cynic complains about a scene all of us have wrestled with. "Don't be surprised when you see that the government oppresses the poor and denies them justice and their rights. Every official is protected by the one over him, and both are protected by still higher officials" (5:8, TEV).

Does that sound like city hall? Still later, Solomon observes: "I saw all this when I thought about the things that are done in this world, a world where some men have power and others have to suffer under them" (8:9, TEV). One person exercising authority at another person's expense.

If we are to keep from sinking into cynicism with Solomon we must look up, not out. Read the following verses. Draw a line from the reference to the statement it makes about God's justice.

Psalm 89:14
Psalm 98:9
Nahum 1:3
Hebrews 6:10

- God won't forget to bring justice to the righteous.
- God won't forget to bring justice to the wicked.
- Justice is a foundation of God's rule and character.
- God will come and judge fairly one day.

day Three

Hope Beyond Cynicism

Let's see if we can find a way to cope with injustice.

Read Ecclesiastes 3:17-21 in the margin very carefully. Underline any traces of hope evident in the midst of Solomon's angry despair.

"I said to myself, 'God will judge both the righteous man and the wicked man,' for a time for every matter and for every deed is there. I said to myself concerning the sons of men, 'God has surely tested them in order for them to see that they are but beasts.' For the fate of the sons of men and the fate of the beasts is the same. As one dies so dies the other; indeed, they all have the same breath and there is no advantage for man over beast, for all is vanity. All go to the same place. All came from the dust and all return to the dust. Who knows that the breath of man ascends upward and the breath of the beast descends downward to the earth?"
(Eccl. 3:17-21).

If you desire to dig deeper...

Read the following Scriptures.
Did Solomon commit heresy when he declared humans have no advantage over animals?

Genesis 1:26-27

_____

_____

Leviticus 24:21

_____

_____

Psalm 8:3-8

_____

_____

1 Corinthians 15:39

_____

_____

SOLUTION 1: INJUSTICE WILL HAVE ONLY A TEMPORARY REIGN

For a rare moment, Solomon actually looks above the sun. He seems to be saying, "Relief is coming. Wrong won't last forever. It's going to be judged under the sovereign hand of a just God. Injustice will have only a temporary reign. Rest easy." Too bad Solomon couldn't stop there. I think he's fed up with injustice, and he lets his cynicism show through (3:18-20). If you press gross injustice to the maximum, if you focus your attention on corruption and unfair oppression long enough, you will come to this exasperating and heretical conclusion.

SOLUTION 2: INJUSTICE REVEALS OUR BEASTLIKE BEHAVIOR

In his cynical rage, the man exclaims that there is no advantage in being a human being. "We're all just like a bunch of beasts, a herd of animals ... and since that is true, our destinations are the same!" I believe Solomon has unwisely and rashly stated heresy. Cynicism mentally confuses us. It angers us emotionally. It numbs us spiritually. It leaves us scarred, bitter, disillusioned, and, for sure, feeling distant from God. That aptly describes Solomon at this phase of his journey.

"I have seen that nothing is better than that man should be happy in his activities, for that is his lot. For who will bring him to see what will occur after him?" (3:22). I believe we are given here a very godly philosophy to follow regarding disadvantages, unfair treatment, and injustice. I think God's counsel, through Solomon, is remarkably on target. I say *remarkably*, because the man had just finished spouting heresy!

Solomon comes back with a solution as his conclusion. "Reject self-pity. Reject revenge. Reject resentment. Reject retaliation. Find ways to discover advantages to your disadvantages."

We can do very little to change our lot. We can only change our reaction. We cannot change our past. I don't care how brilliant we are, our past stands in concrete. But we can learn today to see our past from God's perspective, and use the disadvantages of yesterday today and forever.

THREE QUESTIONS

To help you replace stale cynicism with fresh hope, I want to ask three questions:

Week of JANUARY 16

1. What is your unjust disadvantage? I don't mean little petty irritations. What is a major unjust disadvantage in your life?

   _____

   _____

2. Do you more often display:
   passive self-pity?   OR   active courage? (circle)

   When do you plan to replace self-pity with courage?
   I can't.   I don't want to.   Today, with God's help.

You have been set on this earth as a unique jewel with certain sparkling possibilities when the light of the Son hits it. Imagine the lives you could reach and strengthen simply by being all you can be!

3. What makes you unique? (circle)

   life experiences   personality   talents
   disadvantages   other: _____

   How can your distinctive message impact one person today? _____

   How can it impact the world?

   _____

Disadvantages need not disqualify. You can become significantly used by God if you refuse to let your disadvantages turn you into a cynic.

day Four

The Lonely Whine of the Top Dog

In our examination of Solomon's writing, we have come to a journal entry that addresses the emptiness of those who make it to the top. If you are

> "Then I looked again at all the injustice that goes on in this world. The oppressed were crying, and no one would help them. No one would help them, because their oppressors had power on their side. I envy those who are dead and gone; they are better off than those who are still alive. But better off than either are those who have never been born, who have never seen the injustice that goes on in this world.
> I have also learned why people work so hard to succeed: it is because they envy the things their neighbors have. But it is useless. It is like chasing the wind. They say that a man would be a fool to fold his hands and let himself starve to death. Maybe so, but it is better to have only a little, with peace of mind, than be busy all the time with both hands, trying to catch the wind.
> I have noticed something else in life that is useless. Here is a man who lives alone. He has no son, no brother, yet he is always working, never satisfied with the wealth he has. For whom is he working so hard and denying himself any pleasure? This is useless, too—and a miserable way to live" (Eccl. 4:1-8, TEV).

there, chances are good you'll find yourself nodding in agreement. If you are en route, take notice that such a destination isn't all it's cracked up to be. Those who envy the ones who make it don't stop to think of the price paid to get there. The top dog is usually a lonely, frustrated individual. If you listen closely, you can almost hear a whine from his lips.

Read Ecclesiastes 4:1-8 in the margin. List Solomon's frustrations in your own words.

_____

IDENTIFYING THE VICTIM

The words from this section of Solomon's journal are directed to the senior executives, the high rollers, the top ranking in the military, the shakers and the movers, the "big cheeses." Those are the ones who look successful and appear to have it made. They may appear to be victors, but, more often than not, they are victims.

Solomon is a king. His vantage point is from the top. He's looking around at others in those top positions. He certainly ought to know what it's like! His world is a world of elegance, opulence, and lavish affluence. We are beginning to realize that his inability to find satisfaction in that realm is the major subject of his journal. He's saying, "Let me tell you how it *really* is. Let me urge you to face the truth regarding where all this is leading."

As Solomon looks around, he observes several categories of life—not one of which is satisfying.

OPPRESSIVE CONDITIONS

"Then I looked again at all the acts of oppression which were being done under the sun" (4:1). Solomon says, in effect, "I looked all around my world. I saw in all those places many people who were being controlled by a dominant few. I witnessed many caught in the grip of oppression."

What Solomon sees is a body of people who have most of the money, the influence, the power, and therefore the control of others. What he saw was anything but pleasant. Look at the rest of verse 1: "I saw the tears of the oppressed and that they had no one to comfort them; and on the side of their oppressors was power, but they had no one to comfort them." It's a vivid scene. His reaction to what he observes is equally vivid (4:2).

Week of JANUARY 16

As Solomon looked upon those who had already died, he thought, "How fortunate you are to be gone from this earth, rather than to still be living under this oppression! In fact, better than both living and dead is the one who has never even been born!" It's a strange moment in Scripture when the unborn are addressed (4:3).

I'm sure you've thought about that at times: those of you who are married and have no children; those of you who have gone through the experience of losing your only child and now witness the difficult times in which we live. On occasion, I'm sure you must think that maybe it is better your offspring don't have to endure a society as insane as ours.

Solomon says, "Those who have never been born are better off than those who are now living, as well as those who have gone on ahead." He then continues his appraisal of the world around him, turning from oppressive conditions to a second observation.

Need a break from Solomon's whining? In the margin, list everything you can think of that is good about life.

day Five

The Whine Continues ...

Yesterday we ended with a discussion of Solomon's first observation of life. Today we will see the second and third.

COMPETITIVE DETERMINATION

"I have seen that every labor and every skill which is done is the result of rivalry between a man and his neighbor. This too is vanity and striving after wind" (4:4). Solomon is talking about one-on-one rivalry—fighting and devouring, clawing and pushing. He's describing the outworking of carnal, savage-level selfishness. He's got individuals in mind more than large businesses. It's a maddening, vicious craze to outdo and outsell and outshine the other guy at any cost.

You may have little difficulty identifying with that. You may even see yourself portrayed in this scene. If so, you're not comfortable until you've captured that top position. You're making your moves and you're determined. Some would swing the pendulum to the opposite extreme and suggest, "The best answer is to become indifferent and complacent. Live off the land." But Solomon calls that person a fool (4:5).

A balance is what Solomon is pushing for. Notice the healthy balance in the words of verse 6: "One hand full of rest [that's beautiful in the Hebrew; it says "quietness"—one hand full of quietness] is better than two fists full of labor."

As competition intensifies, we start burning the candle at both ends, and we finally run out of candle. And instead of stopping, instead of evaluating, we simply run faster and farther without facing the music. We refuse to ask where it's all heading or what the ultimate result of this maddening pursuit will be. And our loneliness intensifies.

Which hand best describes you?
❑ **Folded hands, doing little and accomplishing less.**
❑ **One hand, filled with productive work and peace.**
❑ **Two hands, full of nothing but working, clutching, and grabbing.**

PERSONAL DISILLUSIONMENT

This is a scene also characterized by awful emptiness. Solomon says so in his next statement: "I looked again at vanity" (4:7).

He saw a personification of vanity in this "under the sun" observation. Specifically, Solomon saw a "certain man" (4:8). In the first view Solomon has of this old earth, there are *many* people—many oppressed and many doing the oppressing. In the second scene, there are *two* people—one against the other in competitive rivalry. In this third scene, there's only *one*—"a certain man." How significant! As you climb higher on this ladder of "success," you get increasingly lonely; you have fewer friends; less and less accountability. While in the process of acquiring more stuff, you become less involved with in-depth friendships.

Let's take a closer look at that "certain man." According to Solomon's observation "there was no end to all his labor." The tragic truth finally comes out; he doesn't know how to quit. He *can't* slow down. He isn't asking, "Why isn't this satisfying?" and "What's the outcome?" and "Why am I knocking myself out and enjoying so few pleasures?" Solomon exclaims: "This too is meaningless—a miserable business" (4:8, NIV).

Week of JANUARY 16

Once again, read Ecclesiastes 4:8 in the margin. Next to that verse, write the initials of a person who fits that description (perhaps yourself).

A PENETRATING ANALYSIS

The dream of the great society is that we work, work, work; fight, fight, fight; earn, earn, earn; sell, sell, sell; labor, labor, labor to get more, more, more! It's crazy, but there's something so ego-satisfying about being up there. It offers all of those perks we didn't have down below. And by climbing into that cage at the top, we think, "I have finally arrived!"

Solomon says, "Face it, it won't satisfy." Will you hear him? Will you be honest enough to pause in the middle of the ladder and think about stuff others refuse to think about? Don't resume climbing until you can answer this: "If I'm not satisfied here, why do I think I'll be satisfied *there*?"

This isn't designed to be an attack on prosperity. It is, rather, a strong warning against losing a grip on right priorities. Many of those who become successful, wealthy, and famous have a great struggle handling all that. Some are able to keep a clear perspective, but it's tough.

Where is God in your business or your profession? As you climb that ladder, at which rung do you plan to meet Him and come to terms with eternal things? That's why we need the Bible. No other book keeps bringing us back to the truth.

> "There was a certain man without a dependent, having neither a son nor a brother, yet there was no end to all his labor. Indeed, his eyes were not satisfied with riches and he never asked, 'And for whom am I laboring and depriving myself of pleasure?' This too is vanity and it is a grievous task" (Eccl. 4:8).

Read Philippians 4:11-13. What perspectives about satisfaction can you gain from this biblical passage?

Perspective #1: _____ don't determine satisfaction.

Perspective #2: Satisfaction isn't dependent on what you do or do not _____ .

Perspective #3: Satisfaction is only possible through _____ .

Other perspectives? _____

leader Guide

NOTES

To the Leader:

Read Ephesians 2:10. Do you regard your teaching responsibility as a gift from God or just one more thing you have to do? Spend time in prayer, asking God to help you gain (or regain) His perspective about the awesome task you have of leading adults to study God's Word. Thank Him for the gift of being able to do good in your lifetime.

Before the Session

1. Familiarize yourself with the personal response questions in this week's lesson so you can include them in the class session as the Spirit leads.
2. Write "LIFE" on white paper. Cut a rectangular hole in a piece of black paper (the same size as the white paper) and tape it over "LIFE" so only "IF" is visible. Follow remaining instructions in Step 1.
3. Write "wealth, luxury car, large home, perfect health, physical attractiveness" on slips of paper and place in a gift bag. Write the four gifts from Day 1 (page 82) on slips of paper and place in another gift bag.

During the Session

1. Ask: *How is life like a roller coaster? Do you think it's more often life's circumstances or our attitudes that take us on such a wild ride?* Explain. Explain that you are going to travel on a roller coaster with Solomon today as he fluctuates between godly and human perspectives toward life. OR Pass around the black/white paper you prepared earlier and ask participants what they see. Once everyone has viewed "IF," remove the black sheet and pass around the white sheet. Again ask participants what they see. Ask: *Why do you see "LIFE" fully now when you only saw "IF" before?* Comment: *It's all a matter of perspective. Solomon only saw life fully when his perspective rose above the sun. When he remained under the sun he saw only the "ifs" of life. This lesson will challenge us to view life from God's perspective.*
2. State Solomon had a brief moment of viewing life above the sun. Ask a volunteer to read Ecclesiastes 3:11-15. Ask what God makes and lead learners to discuss what they think that means. Give the gift bags to two participants and ask them to read aloud their "gifts." Ask: *Which bag contains the real gifts? Why?* Request participants turn to a partner and share what is good in their labor. Ask volunteers to share with the group what God has done that causes them to stand in awe.

Week of JANUARY 16

3. Comment that Solomon's perspective quickly dipped below the sun. As you read Ecclesiastes 3:16-22 direct participants to underline phrases that demonstrate Solomon was approaching life from a human perspective. Complete the first activity of Day 2. Organize the class into two groups. Direct Group 1 to read Job 21:7-16 and discuss: *How does this passage reflect the same questions Solomon raised? What glimpse of a godly perspective appears in this complaint?* Request Group 2 read Jeremiah 12:1-4 and discuss the same questions. Allow groups to share what they discussed. Discuss the final activity of Day 2 to gain a godly perspective on justice.

4. Comment the roller coaster ride continued as Solomon's perspective again traveled above the sun. Ask participants to state the first solution to injustice from Day 3. Discuss why that truth is important to remember. Say: *Solomon's perspective then quickly dipped below the sun.* Ask a volunteer to read Ecclesiastes 3:19. Discuss the question in the margin of Day 3. Declare: *Just as quickly as Solomon dipped below the sun, his perspective flew right back up.* Invite someone to read Ecclesiastes 3:22. Explain the godly perspective this verse teaches about disadvantages and injustice. Give adults time to quietly consider the three questions at the end of Day 3.

5. Invite someone to read Ecclesiastes 4:1-8. Inquire: *Solomon is at the top, but is his perspective above or below the sun? Explain your answer. Are these words only for those at the top? Why might those at the top especially experience what Solomon expressed in this passage? If someone declared to you it would be better to have not been born, how would you respond?* (Participants may want to use their responses to the final activity of Day 4 to respond to this question.)

6. Review Solomon's three observations about life from Days 4 and 5. Ask: *Have times changed much? What's ironic about Solomon's complaint that the powerful oppress the weak? Are we the weak or the powerful?* Dr. Swindoll exhorted us to move from passive self-pity to active courage—so what are we to do about oppression, vicious competition, and disillusionment?

7. Read Ecclesiastes 4:8b and inquire whether this week's study concluded with Solomon's viewing life from above or below the sun and why. To aid the class in regaining a godly perspective of life, complete the final activity of Day 5.

NOTES

Charles **SWINDOLL**

One Plus One Equals Survival

day One

Survival Counsel for the Lonely

"Two are better than one because they have a good return for their labor. For if either of them falls, the one will lift up his companion. But woe to the one who falls when there is not another to lift him up. Furthermore, if two lie down together they keep warm, but how can one be warm alone? And if one can overpower him who is alone, two can resist him. A cord of three strands is not quickly torn apart" (Eccl. 4:9–12).

Solomon has been talking about the oppressive, competitive, compulsive world of the one who works his or her way to the top of the ladder, becoming the "top dog." Having climbed the pyramid, the leader usually finds he has also become a loner. This person who influences so many is strangely bereft of friends. Solomon, with a great deal of honesty and insight, addresses the loners as well as the rest of us in Ecclesiastes 4:9-12.

Read Ecclesiastes 4:9-12 in the margin. State the theme of this passage. _____

Do you believe that? ❑ Yes ❑ No **Why?**
_____

As you continue your study, compare your reasons with Solomon's conclusions.

The opening line sets the stage with a statement of fact: "Two are better than one." This is for people wondering how to survive in our "dog-eat-dog" culture of ragged-edge reality. He says: "Two are better than one [and then he tells us why] because they have a good return for their labor" (4:9). *The Living Bible* puts it even more simply, "The results can be much better." We gain perspective by having somebody at our side. We gain objectivity. We gain courage in threatening situations. Having others near tempers our dogmatism and softens our intolerance.

Week of JANUARY 23

REASONS TWO ARE BETTER THAN ONE

Solomon mentions three reasons two are better than one.

1. *Mutual encouragement when we are weak* (4:10). In times of personal failure, when we could easily stumble or become entrapped, when we fall on our faces, when we have gotten into trouble, we need a companion to keep us from getting too bruised and bloody. That companion will not walk away. If one falls down, the other can help him up.

Who catches you when you fall? _____

2. *Mutual support when we are vulnerable* (4:11). We need someone when there are elements that we can't change—when we can't make it hot if it's cold. We can't get warm if everything around us is cold. That's the point. We're exposed. We're unguarded. We're vulnerable. And we need somebody to warm us up. Any time or place where you feel self-conscious and your major battle is "How am I going to make it through this right now?" be reminded of verse 11—you are cold and you need help keeping warm. Two are better than one.

3. *Mutual protection when we are attacked* (4:12). There is an adversary we all fight. He is relentless, determined, and clever. He's also invisible. He's called the devil. There is also an entire demonic force that would intimidate us even more if we could see them at work. Even though we cannot see them, we sense their presence and we are aware of their attack.

Sometimes a companion who is near us is able to say, "I think what you're wrestling with is a demonic attack." The adversary may be some other person. At such times companions are essential.

Verse 12 concludes with "A cord of three strands is not quickly torn apart." This is not simply a reference to Christ, who certainly is our Companion. It's a reference to more than just one companion. It may be several—two or three. But this cord of three strands is held with comforting words, or arms around the shoulder, or a visible presence.

Read the situations in the margin. Write a W, V, or A by each situation to identify whether you would feel weak, vulnerable, or attacked in that circumstance. Briefly note how another person could provide you encouragement, support, or protection.

___ First day of a new job
___ First day of a new school
___ Sitting in a courtroom
___ Sitting in a hospital waiting room
___ Sitting in a dentist chair
___ Standing in an unemployment line

day Two

Biblical Examples, Practical Principles

There are times it is helpful to find flesh-and-blood examples in Scripture. Such people never fail to provide hope as they incarnate the theory and demonstrate how it can be fleshed out.

If you desire to dig deeper...

Read 1 Kings 17–19. Note how God provided encouragement, support, and protection for Elijah.

_____

_____

_____

_____

ELIJAH AND ELISHA

Elijah was a prophet with a double problem. First, he was led by God to stand in front of intimidating rulers and make an unpopular prediction concerning a drought that was to come. He walked into the throne room of Ahab and Jezebel to boldly and clearly announce God's message. These godless people sneered and doubted. Nevertheless, the drought occurred just as Elijah had predicted.

According to 1 Kings 17:4-7, what was Elijah's second problem? _____

The brooks dried up, including Elijah's own personal supply of water. He lost physical strength at that time. But before long he was back to face the prophets of Baal on Mount Carmel. He fought fire with fire and he stood alone against their strong words as Jehovah-God made the prophet's words even stronger. The prophets of Baal were ultimately slain in front of him. It must have been an exceptionally draining experience.

While Elijah was physically weak, emotionally vulnerable, and spiritually depleted, Jezebel attacked and said, "You will die before twenty-four hours have passed." Elijah traveled alone deep into the wilderness. The same strong man who stood alone in front of Ahab and Jezebel now prayed that God would take his life.

God never said, "I'm ashamed of you, Elijah." You know what He said to the prophet? "You rest for a while; I'm going to bring you a meal." So He catered this delicious meal, and Elijah went in the strength of it 40 days and 40 nights. Following the long rest and the nourishment from this delicious meal, Elijah came to terms with himself and God.

Week of JANUARY 23

Read 1 Kings 19:14. What was Elijah feeling? Circle all that apply.
Strong   Lonely   Vulnerable
Attacked Encouraged   Defeated

Read 1 Kings 19:19-21. What did God give Elijah?
❑ Victory over his enemies
❑ A break from his ministry
❑ A friend

There's renewed strength as Elijah survives, thanks to the presence of a companion. In fact, he steps into a whole new vision of God's directives for him. In the words of Solomon, "If one can overpower him who is alone, two can resist him."

Principle 1: Companions calm the troubled waters of our souls. There are times your soul will be troubled. And God graciously provides you with a friend. Companions calm the troubled waters of our souls … as Elisha did for troubled Elijah.

NAOMI AND RUTH

Naomi was a godly woman, a wife, and a mother of two sons. By the time the print is dry in Ruth 1, the sons are grown and married. And the biographer tells about these lovely daughters-in-law (one of whom is Ruth) who married Naomi's two sons.

Suddenly a calamity struck the home of Naomi and she lost her husband and her two sons. Naomi was a grief-stricken widow and mother.

In this vulnerable state, Naomi graciously said to her two daughters-in-law, "Why don't you go back to your homes and start over?" Broken, lonely, and fragmented in her spirit, she would attempt to put the pieces of her life together and simply die a quiet death. But Ruth wouldn't let her do it. Read Ruth 1:16. Naomi's daughter-in-law put her arms around her mother-in-law and loved her back to dignity and life.

Principle 2: Companions build bridges of hope and reassurance when we are vulnerable, exposed, and self-conscious.

Read 2 Kings 2:1-6 and compare it with Ruth 1:16. What qualities of friendship were evident in Ruth and Elisha? _____

_____

> "Don't urge me to leave you or to turn back from you. Where you go I will go, and where you stay I will stay. Your people will be my people and your God my God. Where you die I will die, and there I will be buried. May the Lord deal with me, be it ever so severely, if anything but death separates you and me" (Ruth 1:16, NIV).

Charles SWINDOLL

DAVID AND JONATHAN

Saul was a king who began as a good man, yet after a few years in public office he lost this quality. As he led Israel's army in battle, Saul and his troops faced Goliath, the Philistine giant. And Saul was intimidated.

Out of the hills of Judea came a teenaged boy who with only a sling and a stone, put the giant out of commission. The people began to sing, "Saul the king has slain his thousands and David his *ten* thousands."

Saul felt his position was threatened by David. Instead of encouraging David as a fine young warrior, he viewed him as an enemy. He could have prepared David for the throne, but he wouldn't. He could have honored David and promoted him to a position of leadership, but he didn't.

Meanwhile, along came Jonathan, Saul's son. The Scripture says, "Jonathan loved David as his own soul." Again and again Jonathan strengthened his friend David.

Principle 3: Companions take our part when others take us apart. When we have nowhere else to turn, there's nothing like a companion to get us through.

In the margin, name persons who have:
a. been your calming companion.
b. built bridges of hope for you.
c. taken your part when others have torn you apart.

How can you be an Elisha, Ruth, and/or Jonathan for someone this week?

If you desire to dig deeper...

Read 1 Samuel 18:1-4; 20:1-42. How did Jonathan display the three principles of companionship?

a. _____

b. _____

c. _____

---

day Three

What Every Worshiper Should Remember

"Guard your steps as you go to the house of God, and draw near to listen rather than to offer the sacrifice of fools" (5:1).

Week of JANUARY 23

In the margin, list reasons people attend worship. According to Ecclesiastes 5:1, why are we to attend worship? _____

God is saying, "Be alert! Listen carefully. Truth will be deposited in your head that is designed to change your life."

In the first seven verses of Ecclesiastes 5, Solomon unfolds four commands—each with its own reason connected to it.

DRAW NEAR AND LISTEN WELL—GOD IS COMMUNICATING

"Guard your steps as you go to the house of God, and draw near to listen rather than to offer the sacrifice of fools; for they do not know they are doing evil" (Eccl. 5:1). We know from another section of Scripture that "the sacrifice" quite likely is a reference to words, "the sacrifice of praise, the fruit of lips" (Heb. 13:15). For that reason, I suggest that Solomon means "Don't talk so much. Be quiet. Listen well. Draw near!"

The living God is communicating. Be quiet. Learn to hitchhike on God's thoughts. Sometimes those thoughts come in the silence of the offertory or prayer or in the singing of a hymn. Draw near. Listen well.

Read James 4:8. What does God promise to do if you draw near to Him? _____

BE QUIET AND STAY CALM—GOD HEARS THE INAUDIBLE AND SEES THE INVISIBLE

We can be so preoccupied that we simply go through empty, meaningless motions of worship without really hearing (Eccl. 5:2-3,7). We don't respond well because we're not taking it all in. God alone hears the inaudible. He alone sees the invisible. That's the reason we're to be calm and quiet. God penetrates deeply into that which is inaudible to human ears, and He peers intently into that which is invisible to human eyes.

If we're not careful, we drag in all of our problems. And we are quick to dump them out, rather than hear Him out. He says, "Be still."

Read Psalm 46:10 in the margin. In your opinion, what is the main reason we must be still before God?

_____

> "Do not be hasty in word or impulsive in thought to bring up a matter in the presence of God. For God is in heaven and you are on the earth; therefore let your words be few. For the dream comes through much effort, and the voice of a fool through many words … For in many dreams and in many words there is emptiness. Rather, fear God" (Eccl. 5:2-3,7).

> "Be still, and know that I am God; I will be exalted among the nations, I will be exalted in the earth" (Ps. 46:10, NIV).

> "Guard your steps as you go to the house of God and draw near to listen rather than to offer the sacrifice of fools; for they do not know they are doing evil. Do not be hasty in word or impulsive in thought to bring up a matter in the presence of God. For God is in heaven and you are on the earth; therefore let your words be few. For the dream comes through much effort and the voice of a fool through many words. When you make a vow to God, do not be late in paying it; for He takes no delight in fools. Pay what you vow! It is better that you should not vow than that you should vow and not pay. Do not let your speech cause you to sin and do not say in the presence of the messenger of God that it was a mistake. Why should God be angry on account of your voice and destroy the work of your hands? For in many dreams and in many words there is emptiness. Rather, fear God" (Eccl. 5:1-7).

MAKE A COMMITMENT AND KEEP IT—GOD BELIEVES IT AND DOESN'T FORGET IT

"When you make a vow to God, do not be late in paying it, for He takes no delight in fools. Pay what you vow! It is better that you should not vow than that you should vow and not pay" (Eccl. 5:4-5). These are some of the most overlooked words in Scripture, especially in a day of shallow roots and superficial commitments. We'd rather bail out than follow through. As a result, a promise is little more than a casual hope. Whether it's a commitment to pay back $50 or to stay faithful in marriage, the idea of sticking with a vow *regardless* is almost unheard of. Not so in God's eyes!

The command in 5:4 is simply a follow-up reminder: "Keep your word!" God believed you when you took that vow and He doesn't forget it.

DON'T DECIDE NOW AND DENY LATER—GOD DOESN'T IGNORE DECISIONS

"Do not let your speech cause you to sin and do not say in the presence of the messenger of God that it was a mistake. Why should God be angry on account of your voice and destroy the work of your hands?" (Eccl. 5:6). God puts no age limit on serious decisions. God does not ignore or overlook our decisions. Don't come back and say, "Aha! God, You've got to understand. I'm 20 years older and I've learned a lot since then." Keep short accounts. Keep your promise. Keep your vows.

Read Ecclesiastes 5:1-7 in the margin once again and underline commands regarding worship to which you need to pay particular attention.

day Four

Proverbial Principles to Learn

When Solomon writes on money, it's time to take notes. The man knows whereof he speaks. I find three principles in Ecclesiastes 5:8-12 that relate directly to money matters. Read those verses in the margin on page 101.

Week of JANUARY 23

OPPRESSION

The rich tend to take charge and their power intimidates and offends the poor (5:8-9). This first proverb, or principle, has to do with the influence and control the rich have over the poor. The rich tend to be leaders. They are often the best educated, the most influential. They become the officials who run the government.

Those of us who have served our country in the military smile with understanding as we read those words. In my outfit we called it "the system." How often we agreed, "You can't beat the system." The major problem is that woven into the fabric of that tightly controlled system is unaccountability and insensitivity. I am certainly not advocating anarchy. Someone must be in charge. But my concern—Solomon's concern—is the untouchable and often corrupt power that occurs when those with money gain total control.

What do you think Solomon meant to teach us through this principle? Check all that apply.
❑ **Gain power so you can oppress rather than be oppressed.**
❑ **Give up trying to earn money—it will be taken anyway.**
❑ **Don't be surprised by corruption.**
❑ **Don't place too high a priority on money.**
❑ **Other:** _____

DISSATISFACTION

The second proverb allows us a personal glimpse at those who become downright money-mad. *Greed and materialism have no built-in safeguards or satisfying limits* (5:10).

Read 1 Timothy 6:10. Does Scripture teach against: having money OR loving money? (circle)
What's the difference? _____

Solomon uses *loves*—not *possesses*. This isn't an attack against those who possess riches. This is an attack on greed and the materialist. He who loves the abundance that comes with that kind of income will never know the day when he will lean back, smile contently and sigh, "I have enough." Money can buy us tons of comfort, but not an ounce of contentment.

"If you see oppression of the poor and denial of justice and righteousness in the province, do not be shocked at the sight, for one official watches over another official, and there are higher officials over them. After all, a king who cultivates the field is an advantage to the land. He who loves money will not be satisfied with money, nor he who loves abundance with its income. This too is vanity. When good things increase, those who consume them increase. So what is the advantage to their owners except to look on? The sleep of the working man is pleasant, whether he eats little or much. But the full stomach of the rich man does not allow him to sleep" (Eccl. 5:8-12).

Frustration

Reread verses 11-12 in the margin. That brings us to the third proverb. *With increased money and possessions comes an accelerated number of people and worries.* Taken to its logical conclusion the proverb could be expressed in an axiom: More money, more people. More people, more worries. More worries, less sleep.

> **Does your sleep resemble the pleasant sleep of the working person or the worried insomnia of the rich person? (Underline your answer) Read Psalm 127:2. How can claiming the truth of this verse improve your sleep?**

_____

From the outside looking in, we are so impressed with Solomon's wealthy world. But that's only *half* the story. Here is a man with increased money and increased possessions who has more anxieties than ever and more people living off his salary than he would ever have dreamed possible. He can't even enjoy a restful night of sleep.

These are the words of a middle-aged, brilliant, rich king who knows what he's talking about. And it's recorded right here in front of us in his journal. This is the other half. Tomorrow Solomon shares the next series of things he endured. He calls them the "grievous evils."

day Five

"Grievous Evils" to Remember

Read Ecclesiastes 5:13-15 in the margin. The first "evil" that riches can bring is this: *those who have clutched can quickly crash.* Solomon forces us to face that moment we all tend to ignore—the moment of death. I envision a man who hoarded what he had and then lost it through a bad investment. I can see another who fights and wins his way to the top, only to have the bottom drop out of his life as the stock market plunges.

Margin notes:

"When good things increase, those who consume them increase. So what is the advantage to their owners except to look on? The sleep of the working man is pleasant, whether he eats little or much. But the full stomach of the rich man does not allow him to sleep" (Eccl. 5:11-12).

"There is a grievous evil which I have seen under the sun: riches being hoarded by their owner to his hurt. When those riches were lost through a bad investment and he had fathered a son, then there was nothing to support him. As he had come naked from his mother's womb, so will he return as he came. He will take nothing from the fruit of his labor that he can carry in his hand" (Eccl. 5:13-15).

Week of JANUARY 23

And how about the individual in a maddening pursuit of some financial goal, who drops dead of a heart attack? In Solomon's words, he "toils for the wind."

Solomon lists another "grievous evil" in Ecclesiastes 5:16: "This also is a grievous evil–exactly as a man is born, thus will he die." In other words: *Those who live high often die hard.* Solomon continues to show us just how brief life really is.

Read Ecclesiastes 5:17 in your Bible. List three results of a life lived for riches.

1. _____   2. _____   3. _____

In your opinion, what is the relationship between these three conditions?

_____

There are many who once ran fast, lived fast, made a pile of money and spent it fast, who also fell awfully fast and died hard. It's the picture of a person we've seen portrayed on page after page of Solomon's penetrating journal—the touch-me-not, I've-got-it-made, fast-lane materialist who lived in earthly opulence. All for what? An empty, unsatisfying, tragic dead-end street called the grave.

GOOD AND FITTING GIFTS TO CLAIM

All is not darkness and gloom. Before he brings his thought to a close, the wealthy king smiles as he lists three priceless gifts he says are "good and fitting." These gifts are so valuable, money cannot buy them. Read Ecclesiastes 5:18-20 in the margin.

Claim the gift of enjoyment in your life. Joy is a gift from God. Solomon encourages us to enjoy ourselves. In other words, refuse to allow yourself to get caught in the greed trap. Refuse to attach yourself to the dollar sign. Refuse to place top priority on making more, just to make more.

He says, "Enjoy life! Laugh more. Go back to the things that brought you happiness as a child and capitalize on them."

Claim the gift of fulfillment in your work—another of God's gifts. It's not always true that there's a better job around the corner. The greener grass is indeed a myth. Invest more in the vertical dimension of

> "Here is what I have seen to be good and fitting: to eat, to drink and enjoy oneself in all one's labor in which he toils under the sun during the few years of his life which God has given him; for this is his reward. Furthermore, as for every man to whom God has given riches and wealth, He has also empowered him to eat from them and to receive his reward and rejoice in his labor; this is the gift of God. For he will not often consider the years of his life, because God keeps him occupied with the gladness of his heart" (Eccl. 5:18–20).

life, less in the horizontal. Invest your riches for God's work. Invest your time for His glory. Give generously. You'll find a rejoicing in your labor that gives a new dimension.

Read Colossians 3:23-24. List phrases from this verse that can help you find fulfillment in your work.

_____

_____

Claim the gift of contentment in your heart. Enjoyment in your life, fulfillment in your work, contentment in your heart—what an ideal mix!

You're single. You didn't plan to be. So? So, find ways to discover contentment. You're growing older and you're more alone than you ever thought you would be. So? So look for ways to discover contentment. God gives contentment to you as a gift.

Solomon saved the best half for us in his journal. The grievous evils, the warnings, the proverbial principles, and these beautiful conclusions—they have no price tag.

Don't allow the smoke screen of more money to blind your eyes to the truth. There's a lot more to being rich than making more money. Do you want riches? Then listen to Jesus: "Seek first His kingdom and His righteousness; and all these things shall be added to you" (Matt. 6:33).

For the *real* riches, try switching kingdoms.

God has given the gifts; your responsibility is to claim them. Complete this prayer: Dear Lord, I choose

_____

_____

_____

"Whatever you do, do your work heartily, as for the Lord rather than for men, knowing that from the Lord you will receive the reward of the inheritance. It is the Lord Christ whom you serve" (Col. 3:23-24).

Week of JANUARY 23

leader Guide

NOTES

To the Leader:

Make plans to have a class potluck after the worship service one Sunday. Encourage participants to invite friends. Be sure to invite prospects, absentees, and members who teach in other departments during the Bible study hour.

Before the Session
1. Prayerfully choose the teaching steps you feel will help your class explore the material in this week's lesson. In addition, you may choose to engage in personal study of the "dig deeper" features in the margins and incorporate those activities in your teaching plan.
2. Cut 12-inch lengths of all-purpose thread for each participant.
3. Prepare two worksheets: Group 1: Read 1 Kings 17:1-7. How did Elijah feel weak, vulnerable, or attacked? Read 1 Kings 17:8-16. How did God provide encouragement, support, and protection? Group 2: Read 1 Kings 18:16-22 and 19:1-3. How did Elijah feel weak, vulnerable, or attacked? Read 1 Kings 19:3-9. How did God provide encouragement, support, and protection?
4. Provide your church's order of worship (bulletin) for each participant.

During the Session
1. Ask: *If you had a limited amount of paper to write important advice to your child entering young adulthood, what three topics would you cover? Why?* Comment: *Solomon felt the need to discuss companionship, worship, and money in his journal.* Guide participants to compare Solomon's topics with their responses. Remark that Solomon gave good principles for every adult to follow. OR Distribute a length of thread to each participant. Instruct adults to break their thread into three pieces. Ask if that was an easy or difficult task. Then instruct them to combine their three threads together and try to break that length apart. Ask if that was easy or difficult. Comment that you will explore the biblical principle illustrated by that activity.
2. Request someone read Ecclesiastes 4:9-12. Review the three reasons two are better than one. Lead the class to work together to complete the final activity of Day 1.
3. Organize the class into two groups. (Or complete this activity as one large group.) Distribute the two worksheets you prepared earlier and allow groups several moments to answer their questions. Allow groups to share their discoveries. Lead the group to discuss the final

105

two activities of Day 2. If participants are uncomfortable giving names for the last activity, encourage them to simply give examples of how friends demonstrated those principles.

4. Instruct participants to underline principles for true worship in Ecclesiastes 5:1-7 as you read the verses aloud. Ask volunteers to share what they underlined. Ask for responses to the second activity of Day 3. Ask: *How does that describe true worship?* Distribute your church's order of worship and ask participants to note how the worship service allows times for worshipers to draw near to listen. Guide participants to discuss how they can take better advantage of those times.

5. Ask participants to name vows they must make. Ask a volunteer to read Matthew 5:33-37. Inquire: *How can we reconcile Jesus' teachings with the fact that we have to make some vows? What is the main point Solomon and Jesus taught about making vows? What does that have to do with how we worship?*

6. Ask volunteers to explain the three principles Solomon taught about money in Ecclesiastes 5:8-12. Ask: *Why did he choose these three principles; why not more practical money management skills?* Request someone read Ecclesiastes 5:11-12. Ask how those verses illustrate Solomon's frequent declarations that all is meaningless. Write "more, more, more" on the board and ask volunteers to state the axiom Dr. Swindoll made about money in Day 4. ("More money, more people ....") Ask participants if they agree with that axiom and why. Ask: *Is it a new idea to you that God wants you to enjoy peaceful sleep? Why?* Discuss the final activity in Day 4.

7. Invite someone to read Ecclesiastes 5:13-15. Lead the class to identify the grievous evils discussed by Solomon. Invite a volunteer to read Ecclesiastes 5:18-20. Identify gifts believers can claim. Ask: *What does it mean to "attach yourself to a dollar sign"? How can we avoid that? What did you enjoy as a child? How can you capitalize on those things so you can claim enjoyment now?* Encourage participants to volunteer to work with children in church, schools, or recreational sports teams. Ask: *What can children teach us about enjoyment, fulfillment, and contentment? What does Swindoll mean when he tells us to "claim" these gifts? Don't they come automatically? Explain.*

8. Close in prayer that participants will claim enjoyment in their lives, fulfillment in their work, and contentment in their hearts.

Week of **JANUARY 30**

A Change in Scenery

day One

Solomon's Self-Portrait

The next section of Solomon's journal is a self-portrait of the troubled king. He doesn't actually put his name on it, but it's obvious we are looking at the man himself. Read Ecclesiastes 6:1-2 in the margin.

THE SITUATION

The paradoxical situation described in Ecclesiastes 6:1-2 is commonly found among the affluent. God has given him riches and wealth, honor and influence, along with anything else his soul desires. Yet, the man is blocked from enjoying these benefits. We're back to the overriding theme of the book: "This is vanity."

> "There is an evil which I have seen under the sun and it is prevalent among men—a man to whom God has given riches and wealth and honor so that his soul lacks nothing of all that he desires, but God has not empowered him to eat from them, for a foreigner enjoys them. This is vanity and a sore affliction" (Eccl. 6:1-2).

Read 2 Chronicles 1:7-12 in your Bible and complete the sentences.

God offered to give Solomon _____

but Solomon asked only for _____.

God gave Solomon what he requested but He also

gave him _____, _____,

and _____.

Interestingly, the very same "list" of benefits appears in Ecclesiastes and 2 Chronicles. That explains why the description in the opening lines of this section of the journal is probably a self-portrait of Solomon. Don't forget, however, Solomon had honorable and enviable privileges, yet he was not allowed to draw from them the pleasure they can bring.

Today's cynic would call this a "cruel irony," an "unfair twist" that God would give someone these things yet remove from that person the joy those things could bring.

When such events occur, it causes us to evaluate God. See how the verse concludes "For a foreigner enjoys them"? The reason the man can't enjoy them is a foreigner has come and "ripped off" the enjoyment.

The foreigner is not identified. It could signify an *adversary,* some personal enemy who gave the king grief. Perhaps he was undermining Solomon's leadership. The king once had riches and wealth and honor. Now he knows nothing but hiding and other serious consequences.

It could be *sickness.* He once enjoyed good health, but now that "foreigner" has attacked his body and he can no longer enjoy the delights of riches and wealth and honor.

It could be *domestic conflicts.* There is nothing like trouble at home to take away the fun of life. When this "foreigner" enters, joy exits.

It could be *natural calamity.* In Southern California, we occasionally have earthquakes or mud slides or fires that sweep across vast canyons. Other places struggle through floods, tornadoes, hurricanes, and blizzards. The "foreigner" may be a natural disaster, a calamity.

"Foreigners" take away our hopes and ruin our dreams. They cause us to look into the face of heaven and rethink things. That is Solomon's perspective, and he calls it "a sore affliction." In writing this ancient journal, he has been so frank, so painfully honest in his evaluation of life that some people question whether it even belongs in the Bible. This is a man with a cynical eye. He's painting himself, and the colors aren't attractive.

What "foreigners" have challenged your ability to enjoy life? Circle all that apply

Adversaries	**Sickness**	**Domestic conflicts**
Natural calamity	**Myself**	**Other:**_____

Week of JANUARY 30

day Two

Details of the Portrait

As you read about Solomon's quests for satisfaction (signified by the italicized words), underline those you have sought to bring satisfaction to your own life.

Solomon suggests adding a few things to put some color or shading into this portrait. Read Ecclesiastes 6:3 in the margin. He begins by adding *many children* (6:3). Maybe having more children will make life more satisfying. On the contrary! There is something about having a whole family to care for, prepare for life, and release that brings increased and often thankless responsibilities. We don't live under the delusion that our problems are solved by having many children. Solomon would say, "On top of that, this man has life taken from him and he isn't even allowed a proper burial." He adds that a miscarriage is better than that.

"If a man fathers a hundred children and lives many years, however many they be, but his soul is not satisfied with good things, and he does not even have a proper burial, then I say, 'Better the miscarriage than he' " (Eccl. 6:3).

Do you think this man's problem was his children or his expectation of his children to bring satisfaction? (Underline your answer.) What's the difference?

_____

Read Psalm 127:3-5. How can you enjoy your children even when parenting is hard and thankless?

_____

Since having more children isn't the solution to frustration, maybe what is needed is a *longer life*. "Even if the other man lives a thousand years twice and does not enjoy good things—do not all go to one place [wind up in the grave]?" (6:6). If your life is marked by pain, hardship, and tragedy, what good is it to add to it a thousand more years? Those who live lives like that want to live shorter lives—not longer ones.

Maybe what we need to add is *hard work*. "All a man's labor is for his mouth and yet the appetite is not satisfied" (v 7). Work doesn't bring

> "What advantage does the wise man have over the fool? What advantage does the poor man have, knowing how to walk before the living?" (Eccl. 6:8).

satisfaction to an empty life. Hard work doesn't bring relief from depression if there are conflicts that feed the soul with discouragement.

Since none of those things help, maybe we should add a *bright mind, wisdom, a good education* (6:8). This statement seems to suggest that even if a poor man's life is marked by charisma, he is no better off than one who is bright, wise, and well-educated but not satisfied with his existence.

"What the eyes see is better than what the soul desires" (6:9). He's saying, "Come to terms with reality. What you're able to see—the real thing you see—is better than all of the dreams you may hope for."

We need dreamers. They keep us hoping through the tough times. They restrain us from tossing in the towel. When you climb the mountain, the dreamers are up front saying, "Come on!" Those in the rear wouldn't come if they weren't tied on. It takes a few dreamers out front to tell them what it's going to be like, to keep their hopes up. And so it is with life.

The problem comes when we live only in a dream world and refuse to face reality. Solomon is saying, "Don't think by simply imagining amazing thoughts that suddenly your life will become all you imagine. *You need God!*" Solomon comes back into the frame of his self-portrait and speaks from the heart of God as he makes three observations.

> "Whatever exists has already been named and it is known what man is; for he cannot dispute with him who is stronger than he is" (Eccl. 6:10).

First, *God is sovereign* (6:10). At the heart of life's major struggles is a theological issue. Is God in charge or is He not? If we were allowed to slip from this earth in our present state and into the glory of heaven, we would not find one shred of panic or anxiety. We would be stunned at how calm things are around His awesome throne.

"It is known what man is" (6:10). *Mankind is not sovereign.* God is the potter; we are the clay. God is infinite; we are finite. God is all-powerful; we are limited in strength and ability. We may be a lot of things, but sovereign is not one of them!

"He cannot dispute with him who is stronger than he is. For there are many words which increase futility. What then is the advantage to a man?" (6:10–11). The third observation is: *disputing is a waste of time and effort.* As long as I fight the hand of God, I do not learn the lessons He is placing before me. Everything that touches me comes through the hand of my heavenly Father who loves me and maintains control of my life. That's why He's God!

Even a capable, strong-willed king named Solomon had to admit his inability to fight a winning battle against the living God.

Week of JANUARY 30

Record Solomon's three observations below:
1. _____
2. _____
3. _____

As you read Isaiah 45:9-12 and Daniel 4:35 in the margin write the numbers one, two, or three next to phrases you feel illustrate Solomon's observations.

day Three

A Look at Our Own Portrait

Our goal is not to learn a lot of facts about Solomon. It's to enable us to see ourselves better through His counsel … to better understand life and how to deal with it … to come to terms with reality. With that in mind, let's ponder a couple of questions. One of them has to do with life today; the other with the future. Both are in 6:12. Read that verse in your Bible.

Question 1: *Does life seem futile?* We've all wrestled with this one. Perhaps you've even heard some young man say, "I prayed, 'Lord, if I could just go with that lovely woman, I'd be the happiest guy on earth. If I could *marry* her, I'd be twice as happy.' " They meet and later marry. But after a few years, the same man is praying, "Lord, if I could just get rid of that woman, I'd be the happiest man alive!"

We laugh, but we have had similar statements flow from our lips. Once we get it, we find it doesn't satisfy. It isn't best for us.

Have you ever thought if you could have that one certain item, job, or person you would be content?
❑ Yes ❑ No What was that one "thing"? _____

How long did your complete satisfaction last?
One day   A few months
Several years   Until it went in for repairs

Futility rears its head. None of those conditions give us what we are looking for, and we dispute with God. He graciously tolerates us in our circular journey and says, "I'm working on your life. Don't fight Me."

"Does a clay pot dare argue with its maker, a pot that is like all the others? Does the clay ask the potter what he is doing? Does the pot complain that its maker has no skill? Does anyone dare say to his parents, 'Why did you make me like this?' The Lord, the holy God of Israel, the one who shapes the future says: 'You have no right to question me about my children or to tell me what I ought to do! I am the one who made the earth and created mankind to live there. By my power I stretched out the heavens; I control the sun, the moon, and the stars' " (Isa. 45:9-12, TEV).

All the inhabitants of the earth are accounted as nothing, but He does according to His will in the host of heaven and among the inhabitants of earth; and no one can ward off His hand or say to Him, What hast Thou done?" (Dan. 4:35).

111

Question 2: *Are you fearful about the future?* Who knows what the future holds? Sometimes the rapid passing of time suddenly hits us in the face. We're living our lives in a pretty common and predictable manner, then all of a sudden, life rushes upon us.

In the last part of the Sermon on the Mount, Jesus compared the people who were listening to Him to houses.

Read Jesus' words in Matthew 7:24-27. Use the chart to compare the two kinds of listeners.

Since we all hear the same thing, the difference is not in the hearing, but in the acting. Therefore, when the storm comes, one house falls and the other stands for one simple, specific reason: the response.

Does your life seem pretty futile? If so, it's really nothing to be ashamed of. God made us like that. Clay can't shape itself; it needs a potter. Colorful oils can't paint by themselves; they need an artist.

Is your house on   the rock   or   the sand?   (circle)

Depending on that answer, you'll have the answer for your future.

Are you ready to face the living God? (circle)
Absolutely.   No.   I hope so.   I'm not sure.

No matter how much time you have left, the foundation of your life must be solid rock or life *will* be futile. I urge you not to think that reading is the ultimate end of this. It's not; it's following through on the truth you read. Remember what Jesus said about people who build rock-like lives? They *respond* correctly to truth—they act upon it.

Wherever you are, Jesus Christ (the Rock) is ready to take over the foundation of your house. He'll personally remove all the sand and replace it with Himself. He'll take you just as you are, and He'll make you like you ought to be. Your years may be few, but they need not be futile.

Week of JANUARY 30

day Four

Wise Words for Busy People

The terms *wise* and *wisdom* appear almost 35 times in the latter half of Solomon's journey. Why? He is "coming back home." His pilgrimage now takes a turn in the right direction.

As wisdom begins to return to Solomon, it reveals itself in a series of seven "comparative proverbs" that are "better than" their counterparts.

Read Ecclesiastes 7:1-10 in your Bible. Throughout today's study, use those verses to fill in the blanks to complete each of Solomon's comparisons.

COUNSEL FOR THOSE IN THE CRUNCH

Let's take each comparison and get a little wisdom. We may discover how and why Solomon began to find his way back home.

1. *A good name is better than a* _____ _____ (7:1). A good name has a fine reputation. A good name is preferred to that which simply has a pleasant aroma. Nothing is more valuable to an individual than the character behind his or her name.

2. *The day of one's* _____ *is better than the day of one's birth* (7:1). That throws us a curve, doesn't it? We Westerners celebrate birthdays, but we mourn deathdays.

Read Philippians 1:23-24 in the margin. How could one's death be better than one's birth?

_____

Paul and Solomon are saying, "I would rather be beyond this veil of tears and at home in glory, enjoying the presence of the Lord." In that sense, the joyous days following our death are better than all the painful, stressful days that follow our birth. Those who know the Lord in a personal and intimate manner can make such a statement.

The next two comparative proverbs are interwoven with this one.

"I am hard-pressed from both directions, having the desire to depart and be with Christ, for that is very much better; yet to remain on in the flesh is more necessary for your sake" (Phil. 1:23-24).

3. It is better to go to a house of mourning than to go to a house of _____ (7:2). When you get beneath the shallow surface of life, it's amazing how quickly you get rid of the superficial. It's amazing how empty most jokes are ... how hollow the places of entertainment seem in comparison to that which is eternal.

4. _____ is better than _____ (7:3). A joke is quickly forgotten. But we seldom forget a stroll through a graveyard and what we learn there about the great men and women who shaped lives. It's amazing how much perspective is gained when we get a glimpse of life from the back door. That's what Solomon means in 7:4: "The mind of the wise is in the house of mourning, while the mind of fools is in the house of pleasure."

Death gives you wisdom. Those who live their lives suffering from a terminal disease usually demonstrate a remarkable degree of wisdom in the way they spend their time.

Have you journeyed with a godly person through their process of dying? If so, what wisdom did you gain from his or her life and death?

_____

5. It is better to listen to the _____ of a wise man than for one to listen to the song of _____ (7:5). Most of us fail to hear the rebukes of the wise. We find such occasions difficult to bear. But if we are wise, we will not only learn from it, we will be grateful for it. Wisdom can return, but often it takes time and pain and loss and brokenness before its counsel is heard.

6. The _____ of a matter is better than its _____ (7:8). The end of a matter is maximum reality. There are no more unrealistic expectations, no gaps of ignorance, no lack of awareness. The complete picture has developed. I can still hear the wise counsel of my mother's father. Such counsel is better than most advice given to a child because it is coming from one who has been seasoned with wisdom.

7. _____ of spirit is better than haughtiness of spirit (7:8). On this pilgrimage from earth to heaven, one of God's great goals is the development of our inner character, which implies the replacement of a proud spirit with a patient spirit. As that transpires, wisdom has a platform upon which to work. Our haughty spirit pushes wisdom aside, and when it

Week of JANUARY 30

does, we play the fool. That explains why he writes what he does on the heels of this seventh proverb. "Do not be eager in your heart to be angry, for anger resides in the bosom of fools" (Eccl. 7:9).

See how Solomon counsels us against languishing over yesteryear. "Do not say, 'Why is it that the former days were better than these?' For it is not from wisdom that you ask about this" (7:10). Today is today. It will never be yesterday, nor should we try to make it so. God is forever up-to-date, well able to sustain us through tough and challenging times.

Which of Solomon's proverbs of wisdom specifically spoke to you today? Why? Answer in the margin.

day Five

Wisdom: What Makes It So Special?

Solomon doesn't abruptly stop this section of his journal before extolling two specific and all-important virtues of wisdom. It's almost as if he hopes to grab the attention of some who may be teetering on the fence of indecision. First, let's read what Solomon wrote in Ecclesiastes 7:11-14, then let's discover why wisdom is vital to a victorious life.

1. *Wisdom preserves our lives from human pitfalls.* Examples of such pitfalls include:
- With an inheritance comes the pitfall of *pride*.
- With affliction comes the pitfall of *doubt and disillusionment*.
- With the anticipation of relief, vindication, even rewards for doing what is right comes the pitfall of *resentment and bitterness*.

Solomon is correct: "Wisdom is protection."

Next to each pitfall above, briefly state how wisdom is protection against that pitfall.

But wisdom is more than protection.

2. *Wisdom provides our lives with divine perspective.* The Lord our God is ultimately in control. If God has "straightened" something, it's wasted

"Wisdom along with an inheritance is good
and an advantage to those who see the sun.
For wisdom is protection just as money is protection.
But the advantage of knowledge is that wisdom preserves the lives of its possessors.
Consider the work of God,
for who is able to straighten what He has bent?
In the day of prosperity be happy,
but in the day of adversity consider—
God has made the one as well as the other
so that man may not discover anything that will be after him" (Eccl. 7:11-14).

effort to try to bend it (7:13). This divine perspective is designed to replace resistance with relief.

"In the day of prosperity be happy" (7:14). There is no reason to allow guilt to rob you of the joy that should accompany prosperous times. Divine perspective frees us to be happy. "But in the day of adversity consider—God has made the one as well as the other" (7:14). The Lord God is just as involved and caring during adversity as prosperity.

The Hebrew term translated *consider* suggests the idea "to examine for the purpose of evaluating." In the hard times, wisdom allows us to examine, to evaluate with incredible objectivity.

God wants us to walk by faith, not by sight. He won't reveal the future, "So that man may not discover anything that will be after him." God's ultimate design is nothing short of perfect. He's got a plan, but without operating on the basis of His wisdom, we'll panic and run or we'll stubbornly resist His way. This causes me to add these two concluding thoughts. The first has to do with decisions we make; the second has to do with the vision we employ.

Regarding *decisions*—we dare not make a major decision without asking for the wisdom of God. Since wisdom is His specialty, His unique gift to us, it's imperative that we seek it prior to every major decision.

> **According to James 1:5, what can you expect if you ask God for wisdom? (check one)**
> ❏ **Nothing**
> ❏ **The possibility God might help me if He feels like it**
> ❏ **A scolding for asking for something I don't deserve**
> ❏ **The generous, overflowing gift of divine wisdom**

Regarding *vision*—we cannot see the whole picture without drawing upon the wisdom of God. That was Solomon's primary blind spot. The king failed to see God at work. The absence of wisdom ushered in the presence of misery. It always does.

We have not even begun to live if we lack the wisdom God wants to give us. That wisdom is ours, simply for the asking, and it brings us into a new and exciting world! You'll be amazed how clearly things will come into focus. You'll begin to feel like a new creature.

No wonder Jesus referred to it as being "born again."

---

sidebar:

"If any of you lacks wisdom, let him ask of God, who gives to all men generously and without reproach, and it will be given to him" (Jas. 1:5).

Display wisdom by giving glory to God. Describe three specific ways you've seen God at work this week.

1. _____

2. _____

3. _____

Week of JANUARY 30

leader Guide

Before the Session
1. Obtain self-portraits of well-known artists (Van Gogh, Rembrandt, Picasso, Norman Rockwell) either at your local library or the Internet. (It's quite simple to search for individual artists at yahooligans, a children's Web site.)
2. Enlist two volunteers to read Luke 10:20 and Romans 5:2b-6.

During the Session
1. Display the self-portraits. Ask: *If you were going to paint your self-portrait, would you choose a realistic or abstract style? Why? Would you highlight your strengths or weaknesses? Why?* OR Organize the class into two teams. Instruct each team to identify the artists of the self-portraits. Ask what can be learned about someone through their self-portrait. For either option: comment on how Solomon allowed readers to view his strengths and weaknesses through the self-portrait he painted in Ecclesiastes. Remind participants the point of studying Solomon's self-portrait isn't to learn facts about him but to be challenged to look at their own self-portraits and come to terms with reality.
2. Invite someone to read Ecclesiastes 6:1-2. Complete the first activity of Day 1. Ask participants to state the irony of the rich man's situation in Ecclesiastes 6. Ask if participants agree this paradox is common among the affluent and why. Ask what "foreigners" work to take away our joy; encourage them to add to those listed in Day 1. Read Philippians 4:4. Ask: *How can we obey this command when so much seeks to rob our joy?* Ask two volunteers to read Luke 10:20 and Romans 5:2b-6. Guide participants to discuss the joy no "foreigner" can steal.
3. Invite someone to read Ecclesiastes 6:3-8. Ask what Solomon sought to add to his life to ease frustration. Discuss the first activity of Day 2. Ask: *How does the popularity of cosmetic surgery reflect Solomon's "longer life" cure for satisfaction? What would Solomon say to our radical makeover society?* Encourage participants to give contemporary

NOTES

To the Leader:

Read Ecclesiastes 6:2-4. Evaluate how well your class responds to sicknesses and deaths that occur in the lives of your members and prospects. Pray for wisdom to better minister to others in crises and to lead your class to learn from difficult times.

117

NOTES

examples of the truth stated in Ecclesiastes 6:7. Ask a volunteer to read Ecclesiastes 6:9. Ask: *Does that mean we're not to dream of better times? What does it mean? What keeps you going when times are tough?* To aid in this discussion, read Ecclesiastes 6:10 and refer participants to Solomon's three observations. Complete the final activity in Day 2.

4. Ask if participants ever played the game where players try to stomp on each other's shadows. Ask: *How much impact did you make on that shadow when you stomped it? Do you ever feel you're having as much impact on life as on that shadow?* Comment that Solomon felt that futility. Read Ecclesiastes 6:12. Remark that the remedy to feelings of futility and fear is found in Matthew 7:24-27. Complete the second activity of Day 3. Lead the class to identify sandy foundations on which people build their lives. Explore foundations that well-meaning people think are rock-solid but turn out to be sand. Ask: *What is the only foundation that gives life meaning and a future?*

5. Comment that people need a reality check when it comes to the foundations on which they build their lives and Solomon offered that check in Ecclesiastes 7:1-10. Request someone read those verses. Lead the class to rewrite each of the seven comparisons listed in Day 4 from the world's perspective. Ask: *What is gained if you adopt this perspective toward life? What is gained from the biblical perspective?* Read Philippians 1:21 and ask: *Regardless of difficulties, what is the believer's final perspective on this life?*

6. Ask: *How can money be a form of protection?* Request someone read Ecclesiastes 7:11-12. Lead participants to name other pitfalls besides those listed in Day 5. Ask how wisdom can protect them against all those pitfalls. Ask: *What is the greater protection—money or wisdom? Why?* Display a bent clothes hanger or pipe cleaner and ask: *What is the inclination of many people when they see something bent? How do people try to straighten what is bent in life?* Invite a volunteer to read Ecclesiastes 7:13. Inquire how wisdom responds to life situations that are "bent." Ask why people have to be reminded to be happy when life is good and what people need to be reminded of when life isn't good.

7. Encourage participants to ask for God's wisdom so their self-portraits will be of persons who make good decisions and view life from God's perspective.

8. Close in prayer.

Week of FEBRUARY 6

Benefits of Wisdom

day One

The Balance Wisdom Gives

Since Solomon spends most of the latter half of his journal writing about wisdom, perhaps a definition is in order. I've thought about what the Scriptures are teaching on wisdom and I've come up with this: *Wisdom is the God-given ability to see life with rare objectivity and to handle life with rare stability.*

When we operate in the wisdom of God, when it is at work in our minds and in our lives, we look at life through lenses of perception, and we respond in calm confidence. We can lose our jobs or we can be promoted in our work, and neither will derail us. Why? Because we see it with God-given objectivity. And we handle it in His wisdom.

Wisdom is neither academic nor theoretical. It is practical. It is designed to be put to work. This is Solomon's message in chapter 7.

Whether you're a career person, single or married, young or old, this wisdom will work for you. God speaks from between these lines, saying, "Give it a try. Trust Me. I'll give you perspective that is rare and rewarding. And I'll give you stability that is reliable and secure."

Read Ecclesiastes 7:15 in the margin. What statement does Solomon make about himself as this section of his journal unfolds?

_____

"I have seen everything during my lifetime of futility; there is a righteous man who perishes in his righteousness, and there is a wicked man who prolongs his life in his wickedness" (Eccl. 7:15).

He's not bragging, just stating facts. Having "seen it all," the perceptive king realizes the value of wisdom. He mentions three great benefits wisdom affords us. Wisdom gives us *balance*, *strength*, and *insight*. None of these is a natural trait, each is a by-product of wisdom. We don't get these things just because we're human beings. They must come from God.

119

> "Do not be excessively righteous, and do not be overly wise. Why should you ruin yourself? Do not be excessively wicked, and do not be a fool. Why should you die before your time? It is good that you grasp one thing, and also not let go of the other; for the one who fears God comes forth with both of them" (Eccl. 7:16-18).

In verses 16-18, Solomon's words paint a picture of a superpious, overly zealous individual who finds it terribly important to impress others. Read those verses in the margin. This person is a master of external impressions and "presumptuous self-sufficiency"—those little innuendos regarding how much a person may pray and those unbelievably pious looks.

No one is very impressed with our overwise and superspiritual lifestyle. If we've got the authentic stuff, we don't have to say a word. People will notice and they will long to know the secret. In fact, true humility will absolutely cut their feet out from under them.

Read Matthew 6:1-6 in your Bible. Who else is not impressed with a superspiritual lifestyle? _____

What is the reward of those who attract attention with their spirituality? _____

Describe the kind of spirituality God rewards.

_____

"Grasp one thing, and also not let go of the other" (7:18). Really fall in love with the Lord, but don't lose touch with humanity. Study the Scriptures but don't worship the print on the page. Be absolutely committed to making Christ known, but please give the non-Christian a break. Have a little wisdom and tact. See how Solomon's statement ends? "One who fears God comes forth with both of them." There's balance there. We're to fear God, but we are not to lose our perspective.

Tomorrow we will look at the next benefit of wisdom—strength.

Draw an X on the scale below to indicate where your life most often falls.

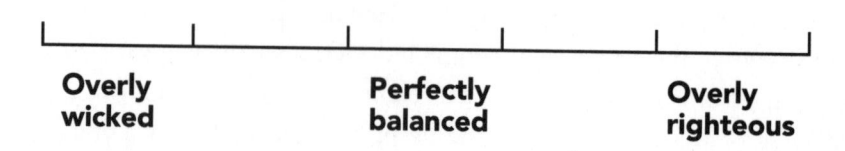

|—————|—————|—————|—————|—————|

Overly wicked   **Perfectly balanced**   **Overly righteous**

Week of FEBRUARY 6

day Two

The Strength Wisdom Produces

We need to be discerning and careful as we attempt to untie the knots of verses 19-22. Read these verses in the margin. Solomon begins by saying that the one who operates in the sphere of wisdom possesses an inner strength to accept painful tensions in life.

The more we glean God's wisdom, the more strength we gain to live with questions and tension. God doesn't issue rules and regulations for every moment. He provides some overall guidelines and principles, then He allows us to make the decisions. By doing this the wisdom of God goes to work, and we begin to learn how to walk through life—which is often full of subtle and unseen "land mines." His wisdom matures us so we can press on in spite of the unanswered questions.

It takes strength to handle the painful tensions of unanswered questions, especially if you have a family. To maintain the respect of your children, you need the wisdom to handle those tensions.

Read in the margin situations most parents must face. Choose at least two of those situations and briefly describe how parents can do the right and wise thing while maintaining the respect of their children.

We've got to live with the fact that there are mysteries. Wisdom gives us the ability to accept that. We don't have to fill in all the blanks or sweep every theological corner absolutely clean. Wisdom gives us breathing and thinking space.

Another strength that comes with wisdom is the strength to avoid the pitfalls of gullibility. Remember what Solomon wrote? "Do not take seriously all words which are spoken."

When admirers offer lavish praise we must not take them seriously *every* time. Wisdom has a filtering system that rejects such verbiage and keeps us in touch with reality.

"Wisdom strengthens a wise man more than ten rulers who are in a city. Indeed, there is not a righteous man on earth who continually does good and who never sins. Also, do not take seriously all words which are spoken, lest you hear your servant cursing you. For you also have realized that you likewise have many times cursed others" (Eccl. 7:19-22).

Current clothes and hair fashions
Body piercing
Popular music
PG-13 and R-rated movies
Organized sports on Sunday
A messy bedroom
Attendance at parties and/or school dances

_____

_____

_____

_____

Neither should we believe every word of criticism. Some people have the "gift of criticism." And they will faithfully exercise their gift by mail, by phone, or face-to-face. And if they can't get to you directly, they will reach you indirectly.

And so, there's a third strength wisdom gives. And that's the strength to resist criticism, or handle it well. Look at the way the ancient king put it in verse 21: "Also, do not take seriously all words which are spoken, lest you hear your servant cursing you."

Solomon mentions the servant as the source of critical words. This person represents someone who knows you very well—someone with whom you work, a "close friend," or a former boss.

Some of you are living your lives intimidated because of criticism. Few people understand that better than I. Criticism hurts me, too. But I am learning that many of those things that once hurt me are better forgotten.

I do, however, want to hear valid criticism. I want to hear criticism from a person who knows me well and loves me too much to let me traffic in wrong. We are wise to hear the reproofs of the wise.

You know worse things about yourself than anyone will ever know. So when you get punched around by the blow of someone's verbal missile, when you are shot at and hit, just remember if the "cursing servant" knew how bad you *really* are, he or she would have much worse to say. So give God thanks that they are hitting just the visible—not the whole truth.

Wisdom can help us rise above both giving and receiving false criticism. And it can also expose pride in our lives if we let it. What we all need is the kind of wisdom we can only find in God. This wisdom gives us the ability to see life with rare objectivity and to handle life with rare stability. It provides us with much-needed balance in a world of extremes; it gives us inner strength in a world of weakness and uncertainty. Next we will look at the third benefit of wisdom—insight.

What strengths of wisdom do you most need right now? (Check all that apply)
❑ **To handle tension**
❑ **To avoid gullibility**
❑ **To resist or positively receive criticism**
❑ **To rise above giving damaging criticism**

Write a prayer in the margin, asking God for wisdom's strength to handle your circumstances positively.

Week of FEBRUARY 6

day Three

The Insight Wisdom Offers

Read Ecclesiastes 7:23-24 in the margin. What is the first insight wisdom offers? _____

_____

The first insight is: *We cannot understand ourselves, nor can we make ourselves wise.* Wisdom is a gift handed to us directly from God. Not only can we not make ourselves wise, we can't even understand ourselves! I hear folks say, "He doesn't understand me." You don't understand you either!

A man once said to me, "Chuck, you are an enigma to me." I thought about his comment for several days before coming to the conclusion that I'm an enigma to *me*, too! I don't always know why I do what I do. Sometimes I don't even know how I do what I do. In Solomon's words, we are "remote and exceedingly mysterious."

The second insight is the toughest of the three: *Intimate relations are compelling, but often unsatisfying.* The writer expresses this insight in verse 25. Solomon talked to men and women. He held dialogues with scholars and people on the street. He pulled together all the information he could get. And what did he find? Look at verse 26.

I think he's saying: "I've probed this to the depths. While with the opposite sex I was seduced into a deep relationship that involved sex and all the other things that go with an intimate relationship and it was unfulfilling." Solomon had seven hundred concubines, and three hundred wives.

Outside of marriage, intimacy arrests the mutual process of discovery. The beauty of marriage is one man with one woman committed to mutual discovery of one another and of life. Let that be broken by an alien relationship and the mutual discovery is lost.

Solomon was also troubled by a recurring enigma (7:27-28). Solomon was saying, "When I was with men and trying to find an explanation, I found one upright man among a thousand." That's another way of saying, it was very, very rare. "But I have not found a woman among these."

"I tested all this with wisdom, and I said, 'I will be wise,' but it was far from me. What has been is remote and exceedingly mysterious. Who can discover it?" (Eccl. 7:23-24).

"I directed my mind to know, to investigate, and to seek wisdom and an explanation, and to know the evil of folly and the foolishness of madness" (Eccl. 7:25).

"I discovered more bitter than death the woman whose heart is snares and nets, whose hands are chains. One who is pleasing to God will escape from her, but the sinner will be captured by her" (Eccl. 7:26).

" 'Behold, I have discovered this,' says the Preacher, 'adding one thing to another to find an explanation, which I am still seeking but have not found. I have found one man among a thousand, but I have not found a woman among all these' " (Eccl. 7:27-28).

Trying to juggle both a marriage and an extramarital affair leads to absolute and certain confusion.

According to Ephesians 5:31-33, how can pitfalls and confusion in the marriage relationship be avoided?

_____

What's true of sexual relationships is sometimes true of close friends. Folks occasionally find that friendships fall flat. That which drew them close begins to erode, leaving them distant and dissatisfied, because they fail to discover the thing they thought the relationship would yield.

These "insights" deal with the relationships every person experiences. The first one involves the relationship with *self*. The second insight has to do with *other people*—a whole spectrum of relationships. And the third is about our relationship with *God* (7:29). *Our basic problems are not above us; they're within us.* They're not with God; they're with ourselves.

Read Ecclesiastes 7:29 and the definition of *device* in the margin. In your own words, describe what the very ones God made upright have done.

_____

We have become creative, but our creativity is misdirected and our devices are destructive. None of our man-made "devices" brings us back to God. On the contrary, they push us further away from Him.

Wisdom is not simply a theoretical, sterile subject to be tossed around by philosophers and intellectuals. Neither is it merely a theological concept to be discussed along cloistered seminary hallways. It is practical. It's designed to work for us. *Wisdom is the God-given ability to see life with rare objectivity and to handle life with rare stability.*

Such wisdom is ours to claim through an intimate relationship with Jesus. In coming by faith to the Lord Jesus Christ, we are given open access to the wisdom of God. It's all part of the package. (See 1 Corinthians 1:30.)

God has the whole world in His hands. Things aren't out of control. The question is not: Will His wisdom work? But rather: Are we putting His wisdom to work?

Margin notes:

"Behold, I have found only this, that God made men upright, but they have sought out many devices" (Eccl. 7:29).

Device—plan; scheme, especially a sly or underhanded scheme; trick. (*Webster's New World Dictionary*)

"God has brought you into union with Christ Jesus, and God has made Christ to be our wisdom. By him we are put right with God; we become God's holy people and are set free" (1 Cor. 1:30, TEV).

Week of FEBRUARY 6

How are you putting God's wisdom to work in your relationships with:

Yourself?_____

Others? _____

God? _____

day Four

Characteristics of a Wise Leader

Solomon's memoirs include a brief section on being a good boss. In our previous study we discovered once again that wisdom is practical, not theoretical. Solomon is careful to give the reader down-to-earth, easily grasped principles (proverbs) to live by. But his concern is that we not leave these truths alone. They are to be lived out!

Ecclesiastes 8:1-9 paints for us the portrait of a good and wise individual who is in a position of authority. His words apply to anyone who is in authority over the lives of others. If you are exercising authority over other people, if you are in charge, then I suggest you take these words to heart. I find at least five qualities of a good boss in the counsel Solomon offers.

A CLEAR MIND

"Who is like the wise man, and who knows the interpretation of a matter?" (8:1). It's a rhetorical question. It is designed to make the reader think rather than come up with "the" precise answer. The key term is *interpretation*. It is from the Aramaic word *pah-shaar*. It means "solution, someone who sees through the mystery of something." It suggests knowing how to explain difficult things, having the ability to unfold mysteries, understanding how to go to the foundation of things. Solomon has in mind an individual who knows *why* things are as they are.

This represents a wise man in any field. You may be in sales. You may be an attorney, a physician. You may be a certified public accountant. Your role may be that of a homemaker and your leadership is over the most influential people of the future—little children today. Why do you raise

---

"Who is like the wise man and who knows the interpretation of a matter? A man's wisdom illumines him and causes his stern face to beam. I say, 'Keep the command of the king because of the oath before God. Do not be in a hurry to leave him. Do not join in an evil matter, for he will do whatever he pleases.' Since the word of the king is authoritative, who will say to him, 'What are you doing?' He who keeps a royal command experiences no trouble, for a wise heart knows the proper time and procedure. For there is a proper time and procedure for every delight, when a man's trouble is heavy upon him. If no one knows what will happen, who can tell him when it will happen? No man has authority to restrain the wind with the wind, or authority over the day of death; and there is no discharge in the time of war, and evil will not deliver those who practice it. All this I have seen and applied my mind to every deed that has been done under the sun wherein a man has exercised authority over another man to his hurt" (Eccl. 8:1-9).

them like you raise them? Why have you set that standard? What's the philosophy of your home? Leaders know those answers.

Consider your area of leadership. Why do you do what you do? _____

Frequently the one at the top is action-oriented and very energetic regarding a product. It's extremely important that the boss not let action outrun thinking. Those who are in positions of authority are, first and foremost, paid to think—to think through, to think about, to think of.

When there's confusion at the top, there is even greater confusion down the line. Those in charge need clear minds.

A Cheerful Disposition

"A man's wisdom illumines him [literally, a man's wisdom illumines *his face*] and causes his stern face to beam (8:1). There are few things more contagious among leaders than cheerfulness. Unfortunately, a stern boss can also infect an organization. It's the all-too-common picture of being stiff, tough, unsmiling, and intense. And this frequently telegraphs a negative mentality.

If your face is stern, chances are good you're not acting in wisdom. If you carry out your role with a stern face regularly and it no longer "beams," you're operating in your own wisdom. If you wish to be a good boss, start with a clear mind. But don't omit a cheerful, charming disposition.

Write M and D on the scale below to indicate the kind of mind and disposition you display as a leader.

|————|————|————|————|————|

Foggy, Frowning   **Clear, Cheerful**

How is God calling you to respond to your personal evaluation?

_____

_____

If you desire to dig deeper...

Read the following Scriptures. What are the sources and results of a clear mind?
1 Chronicles 22:11-12

_____

_____

Proverbs 2:1-6

_____

_____

"Wisdom brightens a man's face and changes its hard appearance" (Eccl. 8:1b, NIV).

Week of FEBRUARY 6

day Five

More Characteristics of a Wise Leader

A Discreet Mouth

If we apply this passage to a place of employment, verses 2-4 are addressed to employees—those being led by the king, or in our case, the boss. Twice the king's "command" or "word" is mentioned. Clearly, the major vehicle of communication from those who lead to those who follow is the *tongue*.

What comes out of a boss's mouth sets the tone of the organization. In many ways, both tone and tongue have a lot to do with employees remaining loyal and cooperative. They respect a discreet mouth. They know their boss cares about such things as tact and diplomacy, sensitivity and compassion. How? The tongue reveals it all.

" 'Keep the command of the king because of the oath before God. Do not be in a hurry to leave him. Do not join in an evil matter, for he will do whatever he pleases.' Since the word of the king is authoritative, who will say to him, 'What are you doing?' " (Eccl. 8:2-4).

Draw a line to match each Scripture with its instructions on developing a discreet mouth.

Psalm 17:3 • Limit what you say.
Psalm 19:14 • Resolve not to sin with your mouth.
Proverbs 10:19 • Think before speaking.
Proverbs 16:23 • Commit to please God with your words.

Keen Judgment

As leaders we have a royal command (8:5-7). An authoritative position *is* God-given. We didn't manipulate, push for it, or play politics to get where we are. It is from *Him*. And He asks that we operate with keen judgment. That includes knowing the proper time to do what ought to be done and having a successful procedure thought through.

Stability under pressure creates respect. A good leader remains calm and steady when trouble is all around.

Effective leaders have independent intuition. They have that extra "sense." They taste it. They feel it.

"He who keeps a royal command experiences no trouble, for a wise heart knows the proper time and procedure. For there is a proper time and procedure for every delight, when a man's trouble is heavy upon him. If no one knows what will happen, who can tell him when it will happen?" (Eccl. 8:5-7).

A Humble Spirit

We all have our limitations. We are impotent to change the wind when it's moving in a certain direction. We can't harness the forces of another wind current and send it in a contrary direction to restrain the wind and weather (Eccl. 8:8). We cannot change or shape the day of impending death. We cannot discharge in the time of war.

Just as we cannot change the wind, neither can we change another person's spirit. No matter what authority God may have given us, there are still many things we cannot do.

A wise leader will allow the Lord to maintain control over his or her power. He will realize that he is gifted by the grace of God to do a job. In humility he will enter the Lord into his decision-making process, problem-solving solutions, and future-planning strategy. Those who follow this leader will continue to feel dignity and importance.

> "No man has authority to restrain the wind with the wind, or authority over the day of death; there's no discharge in the time of war, and evil will not deliver those who practice it" (Eccl. 8:8).

Read 2 Samuel 23:3-4 in your Bible. What causes a humble spirit in a leader? _____

Two Warnings for Those in Authority

It is inexcusable to take unfair advantage of those under our charge. We can rewrite all the rules and call evil "good" and good "evil," but such rationalizations will not deliver us. It's inexcusable to take unfair advantage—no matter how powerful we may be.

"All this I have seen and applied my mind to every deed that has been done under [heaven] wherein a man has exercised authority over another man to his hurt" (8:9).

The second warning is: *Whoever does take unfair advantage of others hurts himself more than others.* A boss who runs roughshod over others just *thinks* he gets away with it. In the long run, he will suffer the most.

Having the right kind of influence is neither accidental nor automatic. It isn't easy, either. Those who model authenticity, dedication, and genuine love for others shape the future of our world.

> Lord I pray that you will fill _____ with the knowledge of Your will in all spiritual wisdom and understanding. I pray that _____ will walk in a manner worthy of You, pleasing You, bearing fruit and increasing in knowledge of You. Strengthen _____ with all power and grant _____ great endurance, patience and joy (Col. 1:9-11).

Insert in the blanks in the margin the name of a person God has placed in leadership over you. Voice this prayer on behalf of that person.

Week of FEBRUARY 6

leader Guide

Before the Session
1. Write Dr. Swindoll's definition of *wisdom* on a banner or poster.
2. Obtain a dictionary definition of *insight*.
3. You will not have time to complete each teaching step. Choose those that best fit the needs of your class.

During the Session
1. Display the wisdom banner and read it aloud. Ask: *Why do you agree or disagree with this definition? How do you observe objectivity and stability demonstrated or not demonstrated in the world?* OR Read the definition and ask those questions after you direct participants to discuss with a partner: 1) Situations where they find it difficult to maintain objectivity. 2) Circumstances that threaten their sense of stability.
2. Invite learners to stand up. Ask what is necessary for a physical body to remain stable as it stands upright. (Be certain balance and strength are mentioned.) Comment that wisdom gives persons the necessary balance and strength to maintain stability. Invite a volunteer to read Ecclesiastes 7:16-18. Ask participants if Solomon's call for a balanced spirituality makes them a little uncomfortable and why. Complete the second activity in Day 1. Ask: *How can people long to know your secret if you express your spirituality secretly?*
3. Request someone read Ecclesiastes 7:19-22. Encourage participants to name the strengths wisdom provides. Ask why believers need strength to live with painful tensions. If most participants have children, discuss the first activity of Day 2. Relate this illustration: Several months ago, a famous pop star fired two of her backup performers after she overheard them saying she didn't look or move as well as she used to. How could this musical diva have benefited from Solomon's advice in this passage? Comment that Dr. Swindoll said he wants to hear valid criticism. Ask if participants feel the same and why. Lead adults to discuss the value of heeding valid criticism by exploring Proverbs 15:31-32; 27:5-6; and 29:1.

NOTES

To the Leader:

Prayerfully review the characteristics of a wise leader from Ecclesiastes 8. Which of those qualities do you demonstrate well as a leader of an adult Bible study class? Which qualities do you need to commit to God for improvement?

NOTES

4. Challenge participants to define *insight*. Read the dictionary definition. Ask why insight is valuable. Request volunteers name the three insights wisdom offers (Day 3). Ask how those insights can provide objectivity and stability. Discuss the third activity in Day 3. Read Isaiah 53:6 and inquire how this verse reflects Solomon's teaching in 7:29. Ask: *Why don't our ways bring satisfaction?* For help in answering that question, refer participants to John 14:6 and Matthew 7:13-14.

5. Remark that all three insights discussed in Day 3 actually point out what is defective with persons' relationships with themselves, others, and God. Invite someone to read 1 Corinthians 1:30 in the margin on page 124. Lead the class to discover how this verse demonstrates how God rectified all three problems within humanity's relationships. [The truth we cannot make ourselves wise was solved by God making Christ to be our wisdom. The problem within us because of our broken relationship with God was put right through Christ's sacrifice on the cross. The problem of interpersonal relationships can be solved when believers see themselves as united, holy people of God.]

6. Ask someone to read Ecclesiastes 8:1. Request participants state the first two qualities of a wise leader. Complete the margin activity in Day 4. Ask participants to read the NIV translation of 8:1 in the margin. Discuss what makes a person's face hard and explore how wisdom actually softens a person's appearance. Invite participants to share examples of leaders who demonstrate clarity and cheerfulness and explain how that makes those persons effective leaders.

7. Read Ephesians 4:29. Ask what quality of a good leader is described in that verse. Complete the first activity of Day 5. Ask a volunteer to read Ecclesiastes 8:5-7. Explain that believers are not to let their troubles determine what actions they take but they are to stick with the proper time and procedure. Ask: *What does this say about the "end justifies the means" mentality?* Complete the second activity of Day 5. Encourage participants to name the benefits of sunlight and rain. Ask how a leader with a humble spirit creates conditions where others can grow and flourish. Invite volunteers to share which quality of wise leadership is the greatest challenge to them and why.

8. Read the prayer from Colossians 1:9-11 at the end of Day 5 as the closing prayer for your class.

Week of **FEBRUARY 13**

Mysteries That Defy Explanation

day One

God's Mysteries

We now come to a segment of Solomon's journal that talks about three rather familiar mysteries: the mystery of unjust triumph, of unfair consequences, and of untimely pleasure. Before we get to the core of Ecclesiastes 8, take a look at what the wise man concluded in verses 16-17.

God's mysteries defy human explanation. Even though we stay up night after night, even though we give ourselves to searching out God's mind in all of God's plan, we are not equipped to explain God's mysteries.

God's mysteries go beyond human intellect and wisdom. The wise man may say, "I know," but can't discover the full picture of what God is about.

All of us have had mysteries invade our lives. No doubt you have had things happen that have shaken and stunned you. Perhaps you've decided to wait until He unfolds the meaning of the drama. And the longer you wait, the less you seem to grasp why. And the further you seek to understand why, the more oblique the mystery becomes. It's marvelous how amazingly relevant God's truth is. We don't have to make the Bible relevant, it is relevant.

Read Deuteronomy 29:29 in your Bible. Mark the following statements True or False.

___ **God keeps no secrets from His children.**
___ **God lets me know what I need to know.**
___ **I have reason to fear the unknown since God keeps secrets from me.**
___ **My responsibility isn't to know everything but to act on what I do know.**

> "When I gave my heart to know wisdom and to see the task which has been done on the earth (even though one should never sleep day or night), and I saw every work of God, I concluded that man cannot discover the work which has been done under the sun. Even though man should seek laboriously, he will not discover; and though the wise man should say, 'I know,' he cannot discover" (Eccl. 8:16-17).

131

THE MYSTERY OF UNJUST TRIUMPH

"I have seen the wicked buried, those who used to go in and out from the holy place, and they are soon forgotten in the city where they did thus. This too is futility" (Eccl. 8:10). Solomon is coming to terms with reality and it's a painful journey. Here he refers to a common experience we have all witnessed: A wicked individual is buried and is given such an impressive funeral that the wickedness of that person's life is glossed over.

It's remarkable what an honorable burial can do for a dishonorable life. The good that men do lives after them and the evil is often buried and quickly forgotten. It bothered Solomon so much he called it "madness." "This is futility," says the king. And akin to this, we see in verse 11 that the unjust triumph.

Let me illustrate. Someone does something bad. You care enough to warn that individual of the consequences. Because he or she did something that was wicked you are convinced "judgment is going to fall." But it doesn't. The person does something even worse later on. And *still* judgment doesn't fall. Because the consequences of evil don't happen right away; rather than turning away from wrong, the individual *intensifies* his wrong. Mysteriously, those who traffic in unjust actions often get away scot-free and even increase their evil deeds. That's the point of verse 11.

We don't like those rules. We like wrong falling off the scaffold and truth standing firm on the throne. Isn't it amazing how some individuals can get away with cheating and deception and dishonor and go right on into more extreme acts of disobedience and dishonor virtually untouched by the God of justice? The lack of immediate judgment prompts them to continue unjust actions.

Tomorrow we will look at two more mysteries Solomon uncovered.

> "Because the sentence against an evil deed is not executed quickly, therefore the hearts of the sons of men among them are given fully to do evil" (Eccl. 8:11).

Read Deuteronomy 32:34-36 in your Bible. When you observe the mystery of unjust triumph, what do you need to remember about:

1. God's timing for judgment? _____

2. The fate of the wicked? _____

3. The destiny of the righteous? _____

Week of **FEBRUARY 13**

day Two

More Mysteries

THE MYSTERY OF UNFAIR CONSEQUENCES

Read Ecclesiastes 8:14 in the margin. What mystified Solomon? _____

> "There is futility which is done on the earth, that is, there are righteous men to whom it happens according to the deeds of the wicked. On the other hand, there are evil men to whom it happens according to the deeds of the righteous. I say that this too is futility" (Eccl. 8:14).

The scene is so familiar and relevant you'd think Solomon lived today. Why is it courageous, godly missionaries are martyred rather than brutal murderers? Why is it a sweet, loving Christian family traveling down a highway is hit head-on by an irresponsible drunk driver who walks away without a scratch, while the family members are all killed? It's a mystery that defies explanation—the mystery of unfair consequences. Who hasn't wrestled with it?

Solomon mentions a third mystery, although it seems out of place.

THE MYSTERY OF UNTIMELY PLEASURE

"I commended pleasure, for there is nothing good for a man under the sun except to eat and to drink and to be merry" (8:15). One could say, "Sounds hedonistic to me. Eat, drink, be merry! Live it up! Go for all the gusto you can get! But wait—don't miss the rest of what he writes: "and this will stand by him in his toils throughout the days of his life which God has given him under the sun" (8:15).

In a world of unjust triumph and unfair consequences, why not? Instead of going mad, attempting to solve all the mysteries of heaven and earth, which cannot be done, the writer suggests a simple plan: "Eat, drink, and happily trust God!" God gives us this alternative to endure life's circumstances. Throughout the days of our lives God will give us the ability to accept and cope with reality even though we're at a loss to explain it.

If you're beginning to need an explanation, it's time to return to those words we omitted earlier: "Although a sinner does evil a hundred times and may lengthen his life, still I know that it will be well for those who fear

> "It will not be well for the evil man and he will not lengthen his days like a shadow, because he does not fear God" (Eccl. 8:13).

God, who fear Him openly" (8:12). There is no way to find any merriment in life, any genuine relief apart from the truth of those words. Solomon isn't denying the reality of sin. Even though sin goes on a hundred times over, even though a life may be lengthened in spite of a sinful lifestyle, and even "though He slay me, I will hope in Him" (Job 13:15). Though I am without answers, yet will I believe in Him.

Check out verse 13. Neither you nor I can grasp God's plan. We don't know how or when God's going to deal with wrong, but we do know God will keep His word. Until then we eat, we drink, we find happiness and contentment in this simple lifestyle. Though evil triumphs, though there are unfair consequences happening all around us, we trust our God to see us through. He is working it out.

In the margin, list the simple things you can enjoy even when life is unfair and unexplainable.

> "I have seen the task which God has given the sons of men with which to occupy themselves. He has made everything appropriate in its time. He has also set eternity in their heart, yet so that man will not find out the work which God has done from the beginning even to the end" (Eccl. 3:10-11).

Look again at Ecclesiastes 3:10-11. Perhaps it would be better rendered: "God has made everything appropriate in its time. He has set eternity in their heart, without which we will not find out the work which God has done from the beginning even to the end." If we miss the eternal perspective, we will spend the rest of our lives wringing our hands and waving our fists heavenward asking, "Why?" and protesting "How dare You!"

It is not the pastor or the Bible study leader or the author who has the answers. We all seek the same answers; we all need the same miracles. Trying to put a spiritual leader in the place of God can only lead to disillusionment and disappointment. It is God alone who has the wisdom to give the answers and the power to do the miracles. In Him is the hope of the riddle wrapped in a mystery inside an enigma.

Look up Psalm 105:4 in your Bible and write it here.

_____

_____

How will you seek God's face today in the midst of life's mysteries? _____

_____

Week of FEBRUARY 13

day Three

Ways to Handle the Mysteries

What do we do with those unsolved questions? What do we do with unjust triumphs and unfair consequences? How do we live realistically in the realm of untimely pleasure? I have three suggestions that might answer those questions:

(1) We must each admit: "I am only human"—and admit it daily. We must not become so impressed with our spiritual redemption that we forget we are human, finite, and fallible.

(2) We must each admit: "I don't understand why—and I may *never* on this earth learn why." We must then try our best, by the power of God, not to let that affect our faith. In fact, we should ask God to use that lack of knowledge to *deepen* our faith.

Read Hebrews 11:8-13 in your Bible. What mysteries did Abraham face in his life?

_____

_____

What one word defines how Abraham handled life's mysteries? _____

The fact that I may never understand why should cause me to be more like Abraham, who didn't stagger at the promises of God through unbelief, but was strong in faith. Every once in a while I remember that a 90-year-old woman and a 100-year-old man had a tiny baby and my faith is strengthened. That's a marvelous moment when we realize that God can do it and *nobody* can explain how He pulled it off. But God kept His word—that's wisdom. And God gave Abraham and Sarah a baby—that's a mystery alongside a miracle. If He could do it then, He can do it now, and we'll wait patiently on Him.

> "'Tis so sweet to trust in Jesus, Just to take Him at His word;
> Just to rest upon His promise, Just to know, 'Thus saith the Lord.'
>
> "Yes 'tis sweet to trust in Jesus, Just from sin and self to cease;
> Just from Jesus simply taking Life and rest, and joy and peace.
>
> "Jesus, Jesus, how I trust Him! How I've proved Him o'er and o'er!
> Jesus, Jesus precious Jesus! O for grace to trust Him more!"
> (*The Baptist Hymnal*, 1991, No. 411.)

(3) We must each admit: "I have no power to change it … Lord. You know what is best for Your child. I wait. I will eat and drink, I will find my joy in You. I will walk in it."

That, dear friend, is the way to live. Through all the misery and the mysteries—trust in Jesus, trust in God, depend upon His Word! When we do that, we too become a mystery, personifying untimely pleasure in the midst of unjust triumph and unfair circumstances. What a challenge!

Read the words of the well-loved hymn in the margin and answer the following:
What promises of God have you rested upon? _____

How will you simply accept rest, joy, or peace from Christ today? _____

How has your life proved God's faithfulness over and over again? _____

day Four

A Biblical Philosophy on Living

Solomon has blasted until there is little more to blast. Now it's time to build! Frankly, I'm glad to see him turn the corner. A body can take just so much negativism. Let's take a look at his more positive mindset.

As you read Ecclesiastes 9:1-10, underline Solomon's conclusions you understand and agree with. Draw a star near statements that will need some explanation.

I have taken all this to my heart and explain it that righteous men, wise men, and their deeds are in the hand of God. Man does not know whether it will be love or hatred; anything awaits him. It is the same for all. There is one fate for the righteous and for the wicked; for the good, for the clean, and for the unclean; for the man who offers a

Week of FEBRUARY 13

sacrifice and for the one who does not sacrifice. As the good man is, so is the sinner; as the swearer is, so is the one who is afraid to swear. This is an evil in all that is done under the sun, that there is one fate for all men. Furthermore, the hearts of the sons of men are full of evil, and insanity is in their hearts throughout their lives. Afterwards they go to the dead. For whoever is joined with the living, there is hope; surely a live dog is better than a dead lion. For the living know they will die; but the dead do not know anything, nor have they any longer a reward, for their memory is forgotten. Indeed their love, their hate, and their zeal have already perished, and they will no longer have a share in all that is done under the sun. Go then, eat your bread in happiness, and drink your wine with a cheerful heart; for God has already approved your works. Let your clothes be white all the time, and let not oil be lacking on your head. Enjoy life with the woman whom you love all the days of your fleeting life which He has given to you under the sun; for this is your reward in life, and in your toil in which you have labored under the sun. Whatever your hand finds to do, verily, do it with all your might; for there is no activity or planning or wisdom in Sheol where you are going (Eccl. 9:1-10).

Solomon is coming to terms with reality. Thus far, his journal has been devoted to an exposé of emptiness. In effect he is saying, "I've tried all those things and they do not satisfy. Let me introduce to you that which has substance—the things you can count on. I know, I've been there!" Then he presents to us the major realities that give life definition and meaning.

THE SOVEREIGN HAND OF GOD

Among the inescapable, inevitable realities, first and foremost there is the sovereign hand of God (9:1). Regardless of rank, status, color, creed, age, heritage, intelligence, or temperament, "the hand of God" is upon us. Nothing is out of control.

Being in the hand of God is not synonymous with or a guarantee for being economically prosperous, physically healthy, protected from pain, enjoying a trouble-free occupation, and having everyone smile and appreciate us. What does help is the knowledge that behind whatever happens is a God who cares, who hasn't lost a handle on the controls.

The picture isn't complete yet. There's another inescapable factor that various human philosophies would try to diminish.

"Righteous men, wise men, and their deeds are in the hand of God. Man does not know whether it will be love or hatred; anything awaits him" (Eccl. 9:1).

> "It is the same for all. There is one fate for the righteous and for the wicked; for the good, for the clean, and for the unclean; for the man who offers a sacrifice and for the one who does not sacrifice. As the good man is, so is the sinner; as the swearer is, so is the one who is afraid to swear. This is an evil in all that is done under the sun, that there is one fate for all men" (Eccl. 9:2-3).

THE ABSOLUTE CERTAINTY OF DEATH

Death awaits us all (9:2-3). You can count on it. As Euripides, a Greek poet, once said, "Death is the debt we all must pay." This theme is repeated over and over again throughout Scripture.

Look up the Scriptures below. Next to each one, write the letter of the statement it makes about death.

___ **Genesis 3:19** A. Death entered the world through sin and spread to all humanity.

___ **Psalm 89:48** B. People are made from dust and their bodies will return to dust.

___ **Romans 5:12** C. Your life will fade away as quickly as morning mist.

___ **James 4:14** D. No one can escape death.

When we give attention to Solomon's journal, we are reading the "fine-hammered steel" of a man telling us the truth, not the least of which is the absolute certainty of death.

If you think the first two realities were tough to handle, here's the third.

EVIL AND INSANITY RESIDE IN THE HUMAN HEART

"The hearts of the sons of men are full of evil, and insanity is in their hearts throughout their lives. Afterwards they go to the dead" (Eccl. 9:3). We've heard about the doctrine of depravity, but not the doctrine of insanity, right? Honestly, have you ever seen this in Scripture before? Lurking in the human heart is a permanent mixture of evil and insanity.

But the fourth reality will help immensely as we try to cope with the world in which we live.

THERE IS HOPE FOR THE LIVING

I'm so glad we have finally arrived at something positive and affirming—hope for the living (Eccl. 9:4-6). There is nothing as encouraging as hope. It brings light into an otherwise dark chamber. Solomon quotes an Arabic proverb familiar to him but not to us: "A live dog is better than a dead lion." In our day, it doesn't have the ring of truth that it had then. Today, our pets are pampered. In those days, dogs were diseased mongrels that ran in packs through city streets. People feared them. Nevertheless, Solomon says that a live dog is better than the king of the jungle who's

> "For whoever is joined with the living, there is hope; surely a live dog is better than a dead lion. For the living know they will die; but the dead do not know anything, nor have they any longer a reward, for their memory is forgotten. Indeed their love, their hate, and their zeal have already perished, and they will no longer have a share in all that is done under the sun" (Eccl. 9:4-6).

Week of FEBRUARY 13

dead. Can you guess why? The king of the jungle, if he's dead, has no hope. As long as there's life, there's a dream, there's the anticipation of a new plan, there's love, there's purpose. Along with life comes *hope*.

As you go throughout your daily routine, pause occasionally to thank God for life and hope.

day Five

How to Live 365 Days a Year

The point is clear: If we are alive, we have hope. The next section of Solomon's journal addresses the other side, and it's wonderfully bright. In fact, I find the words in Ecclesiastes 9:7-10 contagiously enthusiastic. I think they offer a superb credo, a great way to live.

Verse 7 begins, "Go then." Solomon is saying, "I don't want you to just sit there and sigh as you read over my earlier remarks. I don't want you to groan and say, 'Ahhh, I suppose that's life?'" He wants us to get on with it!

LIVE HAPPILY WHEREVER YOU ARE

Since there's hope for the living, Solomon completes the thought with "eat your bread in happiness, drink your wine with a cheerful heart; for God has already approved your works."

Not many people would give us that advice today. This is one of the first glimmers of the new covenant back in the Old Testament, and it's wonderful. Life is not a sentence leveled against us. We are not designed to pine away under a ton of guilt. God is not angry with us. He is satisfied, contented, and at peace. What a wonderful hope for believers! You and I are to live happily wherever we are. So, live it up!

I can just hear someone say, "That's what I want! I've been waiting for the green light—free and easy hedonism, here I come!" Read verse 8.

We have to dress in white? That's not the point, anymore than we are expected to let oil keep running down our heads. This is one of many symbolic statements in Scripture.

"Go then, eat your bread in happiness, and drink your wine with a cheerful heart; for God has already approved your works. Let your clothes be white all the time; and let not oil be lacking on your head. Enjoy life with the woman whom you love all the days of our fleeting life which He has given to you under the sun; for this is your reward in life, and in your toil in which you have labored under the sun. Whatever your hand finds to do, verily, do it with all your might; for there is no activity or planning or wisdom in Sheol where you are going" (Eccl. 9:7-10).

"Let your clothes be white all the time, and let not oil be lacking on your head" (Eccl. 9:8).

Read Revelation 3:4. What does white symbolize?
Cold   Purity   Fear   Righteousness

Read 1 Samuel 16:13. What does oil symbolize?
Filth   Holy Spirit   Power   Wealth

WALK IN PURITY AND IN THE POWER OF THE SPIRIT

The idea is to live a pure and godly life, walking in righteousness and letting the power of the Spirit flow through us. Solomon's counsel continues: "Enjoy life with the woman whom you love all the days of your fleeting life" (8:9).

Husbands, the target of your love is the woman God gave you; enjoy her immensely! And wives, "Enjoy life with the [man] whom you love all the days of your fleeting life which He has given to you under the sun." Isn't that great counsel? Have a blast in that marriage of yours!

THROW YOURSELF FULLY INTO ... WHATEVER

"Whatever your hand finds to do, verily do it with all your might ..." (8:10). I see no restrictions here. A lot of people can't seem to take this for what it really says. The main thing they "throw themselves into" is the bed at night, totally exhausted. This is talking about our hands, our hearts, our whole lives! This is saying, "Throw yourself fully into all of life. Don't hold back. Don't save your strength. Don't put off living. Have a blast now! For there's no activity or planning or wisdom in Sheol where you are going" (8:10). The time to live is *now*!

There's a contagious enthusiasm in the way we're to live. Life becomes exciting, infectiously happy. There are so many grim prophets who seem afraid of having a blast—almost as if such a life is suspect. No wonder more people aren't interested in our Christianity!

Don't play a part in that. Live life to its fullest! Have a blast!

What advice of Solomon's do you most need to heed? (Check all that apply.)
❑ Get on with life!
❑ Bloom where I am planted.
❑ Have a blast in my marriage.
❑ Live in purity and the Holy Spirit's power.
❑ Don't hold back—live out loud!

Week of FEBRUARY 13

leader Guide

Before the Session
1. Obtain a jigsaw puzzle. (Check your church's early childhood department. Puzzles for ages 5-8 years would probably work best.)
2. Enlist two volunteers to read Job 13:15 and Daniel 3:16-18.

During the Session
1. Ask participants if they like mystery novels or movies and why. Ask participants if they like mysteries in their personal lives and why. OR Organize the class into several small groups. Distribute several puzzle pieces to each group (or an entire small puzzle). Allow them 30 seconds to try to put the puzzles together. Ask: *Can life's puzzles be solved as quickly as these puzzles? Why? What puzzles you about life?*
2. Comment that Solomon was puzzled by three mysteries of life. Ask participants to name those mysteries. Request a volunteer read Ecclesiastes 8:10. Inquire what is unjust about the situation described in that verse. Read aloud Galatians 1:10 and ask how that verse can encourage believers when the unjust win the world's approval. Invite someone to read Ecclesiastes 8:11 and 14. Ask what emotions participants experience when they observe good people suffer while evil people continually get away with wrong behavior. Acknowledge these are mysteries that defy explanation. Invite volunteers to share Scripture verses that have empowered them to handle circumstances that cannot be explained. You may need to stimulate their thoughts and discussion by reading Ecclesiastes 8:12-13 and Isaiah 55:8-9 or by discussing the final activity of Day 1.
3. Ask someone to read Ecclesiastes 8:15-17. Guide participants to explore Solomon's advice for dealing with painful mysteries. Invite someone to read Deuteronomy 29:29. Lead the class to determine how they could use this verse to counsel someone who's trying desperately to solve life's mysteries. Encourage participants to be content to take the puzzling pieces of life one by one without trying to fit them together in some sort of explainable plan. One way they can do that is by taking pleasure in simple things. Allow volunteers to

NOTES

To the Leader:

A teaching plan is like a skeleton. It provides the framework or backbone for the class session. It is the leader's responsibility to add flesh, spirit, and personality to the lesson through personal Bible study, preparation, application, and spiritual transformation.

NOTES

share their responses to the second activity of Day 2. Comment: *When we find pleasure in simple things, even when life is unjust and unfair, we become the puzzle—the mystery. Then persons who enjoy mysteries and puzzles will seek us out and want to know our secret!*

4. Write "Give It Up!" on the board and declare that is a believer's secret. Encourage adults to explore the material in Day 3 to discover three things persons must give up if they are to enjoy life even when life is a mystery. Help participants understand they must give up their sinful desire to be more than human, to be God. Remind them of Solomon's admonition to remember our place in Ecclesiastes 5:2. Secondly, persons must give up their "right" or desire to know why. Ask how not knowing why can actually increase a believer's faith. Invite two volunteers to read Job 13:15 and Daniel 3:16-18. Ask if these four men expressed faith in who God is or in what God could do. Inquire: *What's the difference? Which kind of faith helps you handle life's mysteries? Why?* Explain that persons must also give up the drive to change things; they must wait on God. Read the hymn in the margin on page 136. Invite volunteers to share other hymns or choruses that encourage them to trust and wait on Jesus.

5. Instruct participants to follow the directions to the first activity in Day 4 as you read aloud Ecclesiastes 9:1-10. Allow volunteers to share why they agreed with certain statements. Encourage participants to draw on their personal study of Days 4 and 5 to help one another grasp the meaning of the statements they starred.

6. Allow volunteers to share which of Solomon's philosophies on living in Day 5 are the most challenging to them and why. Ask a volunteer to read Colossians 3:23. Discuss the incentive believers have to throw themselves fully into everything they do and why that added incentive should make a difference.

7. Request someone read again Ecclesiastes 9:1. Inquire why a true philosophy for living must begin with the acknowledgement of God's sovereignty. Read aloud Isaiah 49:15-16. Encourage adults that, despite life's mysteries, they can always be assured of God's love and care for them because they are in the sovereign hand of God. Close in prayer.

Week of FEBRUARY 20

An Objective View of the Rat Race

day One

Some "Under the Sun" Counsel

I'm so grateful for the ancient journal which Solomon wrote and God preserved. Again and again it says, "Live realistically. Face life as it *is*, not as you *think* it is or as you *wish* it were. This *is* life! Face it. And enjoy it." It grants us the right to squeeze every enjoyment out of life.

What do you think it takes to be successful in today's world? _____

_____

A large number of people would say the way to succeed is to increase speed, get stronger, be competitive, think more cleverly and have a visionary strategy. Get up earlier. Go to bed later. Make work a top priority. Don't get sentimental about stuff like children, marriage, home, and the family. All that will have to wait. And religion? Leave that for the over-the-hill gang and preachers. Don't get too involved in it because, after all, the race to success is for the swift, the strong, and the clever.

It all sounds so logical, so appealing. But there is another side to be considered. Look at verse 11. Success is not what you think! The maddening rat race is for empty-headed rats—not intelligent, clear-thinking people. The philosophy of our day will attempt to suck us in and convince us that we've got to be stronger, more competitive, more clever, and even more manipulative. Otherwise, we won't be successful. Don't believe it!

Why would Solomon be so emphatic as he denies the age-old ideas regarding getting ahead?

> "I again saw under the sun that the race is not to the swift and the battle is not to the warriors, and neither is bread to the wise nor wealth to the discerning nor favor to men of ability; for time and chance overtake them all" (Eccl. 9:11).

Underline the statement in Ecclesiastes 9:11 that explains why true success doesn't come to the most competitive or aggressive.

We're back to another "mystery," aren't we? That which appears to have the most speed, the greatest power, and the strongest influence hangs on the thin threads of time and chance.

Once again we're talking about the sovereign hand of God. Even though we may not read a lot about God's sovereignty in the daily news, it is at work. In the final analysis His time and His plan (called "chance" by Solomon) win out. The hand of God has a way of bringing about contrasting results rather than expected and logical results.

No, the race is not always to the swift. The strong are not always the strongest. Those most clever and competitive aren't always the wealthiest. Look at verse 12. We may think we're powerful, but we're "like fish caught in a treacherous net" or "like birds trapped in a snare." The writer is drawing an analogy—"So the sons of men are ensnared at an evil time when it suddenly falls on them."

Everything is moving in a certain direction. It's predictable. It's planned. Success is coming. Momentum is increasing. Soon all the pieces will fall together. But *suddenly* (and this is the key word) God has a way of bringing all our plans to an abrupt halt.

Solomon is now prompted to address this whole issue by telling a parable (9:13-15).

**Read Solomon's parable in the margin.
Who was the truly successful person in this parable?
The great king   The poor wise man (circle)**

What do you find ironic about the success of the poor man? _____

Solomon's story is more than a simple account of a city under siege. It's a scene that communicates the importance of wisdom. I don't believe it's farfetched to suggest that the city in the parable represents a life under pressure—people like you and me in any generation, living our lives, realizing a very loud and powerful enemy is present whose desire is twofold: initially to seduce us and ultimately to destroy us.

"Man does not know his time: like fish caught in a treacherous net, and birds trapped in a snare, so the sons of men are ensnared at an evil time when it suddenly falls on them" (Eccl. 9:12).

"This I came to see as wisdom under the sun, and it impressed me. There was a small city with few men in it and a great king came to it, surrounded it, and constructed large siegeworks against it. But there was found in it a poor wise man and he delivered the city by his wisdom. Yet no one remembered that poor man" (Eccl. 9:13-15).

Week of FEBRUARY 20

day Two

Some "Above the Sun" Wisdom

Let's consider four or five statements of wisdom that come from this parable. We've already seen one: *Human ability cannot guarantee genuine success.*

Read John 10:10 and 1 Peter 5:8 in your Bible. What terms are used to describe your enemy?

_____

What goals does the enemy have for your life?

_____

But the approaching enemy won't tell us that! The enemy's desire is to convince us that human ability is what's needed to protect the city. We can build a wall as high as we wish, but if we listen long enough to the shouting of the enemy, the walls will cave in.

Can you hear the shouts? "Place all your attention on human ability. Give up those sentimental things like eternal priorities and lifelong commitments and a relationship with Christ. Buy into the system!" It seems all right. But human ability cannot guarantee genuine success.

Solomon gives us another statement of wisdom in verse 16: "So I said, 'Wisdom is better than strength.'" *Strength is more impressive yet less effective than wisdom.* If we stand strength alongside wisdom, strength will get the public's vote practically every time. We're impressed with it. It is intimidating. It fits our times. How is strength more impressive? It's always going faster; getting stronger; getting smarter, more clever, more competitive, more skillful. But in verse 16 are the words from the wise yet poor man (whom you'll recall is not remembered). His words, nevertheless, live on.

There's a third piece of counsel given as verse 16 continues: "But the wisdom of the poor man is despised and his words are not heeded." *Wise counsel is never popular, rarely obeyed, and seldom remembered.*

Do you see what this is about? This isn't a simple little story about a village. This is a parable offering insight about life. And the poor man is not some big-time professional counselor who is talking with us. It's the inner heart, the conscience, the spirit within us. It's that which pulsates with Scripture—that which is in touch with the timeless sage called the Spirit of God. It is the inner man that quietly waits to be obeyed.

The fourth statement of wisdom is in verse 17: *Human rulers will always outshout wise counselors, and fools prefer the former.* Wise counselors give accurate yet quiet counsel, but fools prefer to hear the advice of loud rulers.

> "The words of the wise heard in quietness are better than the shouting of a ruler among fools" (Eccl. 9:17).

You may be wrestling with doing what is right. You may be struggling with ethics. The advancing enemy on the outside says, "I'll give you a plan that will work! Listen to me! Ignore all that biblical stuff—it won't work in this day and age. The race is for the swift. It's for the strong. I'll even give you a plan where you can rationalize wrong. You can bend it so you won't even have a guilty conscience. I'll provide you with new ways to think ... to reason ... to rationalize. Just let me over the wall." He shouts loudly and convincingly. You may even have a few friends encouraging you, who say, "It's okay, relax. You're too uptight."

But deep within, the poor wise man is whispering, "Don't do that." The enemy is always louder and more convincing than the quiet wise man. If you're not a fool, you'll listen to the wise (9:18).

> "Wisdom is better than weapons of war, but one sinner destroys much good" (Eccl. 9:18).

Here's the fifth piece of advice. *Constructive words of wisdom are no match for destructive weapons of war.* It is our tendency to choose the path of least resistance and to find so-called authorities who help us rationalize wrong, who offer us other definitions of and alternatives to truth.

If we are Christians, there is a quiet voice deep within our spirits.

Read 1 Kings 19:11-13 and Isaiah 30:21 in your Bible and complete the sentence: The quiet voice within believers belongs to _____ and it tells us _____.

It is the voice of the Spirit of God, prompting us to turn to God's Book as our unerring guide. He won't shout. He won't use force. He won't even threaten. He speaks softly and waits patiently to be heard and obeyed.

Listen to God, even if His counsel is painful. Even if you find few people who agree with you, if God says it, do it. Not until you do will you find relief and recovery. Only then can you truly come to terms with reality.

Week of **FEBRUARY 20**

day Three

Wisdom and Folly

As we pick up the story, we find ourselves coming upon an interlude—sort of a transition. Another body of truth is about to be introduced. Ecclesiastes 10:1-11 may be one of the most difficult to understand. As you read it, you'll see what I mean. Solomon has several contrasts in mind, each one being an illustration of the contrast between wisdom and folly.

ADVANTAGES VS. DISADVANTAGES

There's this elegant vase of costly perfume with flies in it. If the dead insects are left, the entire jar gets a pungent odor. He's not referring simply to perfumer's oil and actual dead flies. He seems to have in mind a life of folly. Even a little bit of folly, if it remains in a life of dignity and honor, will cast a dark shadow over all the honor of what once characterized that life. If the wrong isn't cleared up, it's ruined—it "stinks."

"Dead flies make a perfumer's oil stink, so a little foolishness is weightier than wisdom and honor" (Eccl. 10:1).

What seemingly insignificant foolish behavior is "stinking up" the wisdom you possess? (circle)

Leisure activities	**Speech**	**Eating habits**
Spending habits	**Worry**	**Other:** _____

Folly is a term we don't use that often, but it is used frequently in Scripture. It suggests a lack of good sense, lack of foresight, failing to realize the consequences of a stupid act *before* it occurs. Scripture calls that "folly" or "foolishness." And it can happen in our day just as it happened in Solomon's day.

"A wise man's heart directs him toward the right, but the foolish man's heart directs him toward the left" (10:2). "Right" represents that which is worthy of our effort and pursuit. Scripture is replete with occasions depicting the right hand as where God is. A wise person goes God's way. A fool is encouraged by the excitement and the adventure of wrong.

"A wise man's heart directs him toward the right, but the foolish man's heart directs him toward the left" (Eccl. 10:2).

> "Even when the fool walks along the road his sense is lacking, and he demonstrates to everyone that he is a fool" (Eccl. 10:3).

> "If the ruler's temper rises against you, do not abandon your position, because composure allays great offenses" (Eccl. 10:4).

> "There is an evil I have seen under the sun, like an error which goes forth from the ruler—folly is set in many exalted places while rich men sit in humble places. I have seen slaves riding on horses and princes walking like slaves on the land" (Eccl. 10:5-7).

> "He who digs a pit may fall into it, and a serpent may bite him who breaks through a wall. He who quarries stones may be hurt by them; and he who splits logs may be endangered by them. If the axe is dull and he does not sharpen its edge, then he must exert more strength. Wisdom has the advantage of giving success" (Eccl. 10:8-10).

Read Ecclesiastes 10:3. Underline what the fool does when he takes his own road.

This next part moves into the social life. This is where tragedy strikes. If a fool lived alone, it would be bad enough; but he or she relates to a world. And the ripples created by that life are frequently disastrous.

HUMILITY AND PATIENCE VS. POPULARITY AND PARTIALITY

In verse 4 Solomon tells us how to live wisely with an unwise boss. "If the ruler's temper rises against you, do not abandon your position." That could mean, "Don't change your style. Fight back with the same kind of temper." But it probably means, "Don't quit your job in a fit of anger."

There are occasions when even an offended employee will realize that a quiet spirit is the best way to handle this situation. With wisdom we respond under quiet control and our composure disarms his offense. Even with a hot-headed boss, we can soar like eagles.

Another evil is addressed in verses 5-7 that has to do with someone responsible for the many people under his authority. Understand that the one who has the ability, the discernment, the wherewithal to handle authority and make intelligent decisions is, of all things, treated like a slave. It's what we might call, for lack of better terms, "political inequity."

Unfortunately, fools are not limited to places of low esteem. Sometimes they become governors and senators, mayors and civic leaders, principals of schools and pastors of churches. They can even be the ones who own the business and call the shots when, in fact, there are some under their authority who are far better qualified to lead. Yet they are not being given a chance to do so. Maybe God wants us to see just how foolish we can be when left to our own ways.

INEVITABLE RISKS VS. INEXCUSABLE STUPIDITY

In verses 8-10 we happen upon some very unusual statements. What do they mean? If we fail to see the symbolism here, we'll find ourselves woefully confused. What we have here are several dangerous situations.

Read Ecclesiastes 10:8-10 in the margin. Next to each situation listed at the top of the next page, write the potential danger.

Week of FEBRUARY 20

Situation	Danger
1. Digging pits	1. _____
2. Breaking through a wall	2. _____
3. Quarrying stones	3. _____
4. Splitting logs	4. _____
5. Chopping wood	5. _____

The fool habitually "digs a pit" for someone else to fall into and then invariably gets hurt more than the victim. Initially, it looks like they're going to win, but ultimately they are the ones who lose. Today, we call it "poetic justice." But fools can't understand this. They continue to live their lives taking advantage of people, either not knowing or, worse, not caring that they themselves are the losers in the process. Solomon's hope is to awaken us to the advantages of wisdom.

day Four

Advantages of Wisdom

Wisdom prepares the way for success. I don't know of a hotter subject today than success. Magazine articles, books, seminars, and sermons promote it. But success is seldom linked with wisdom.

It may not give us popularity and wealth, and we may not be the most respected in our fields or have the most significant voice in the company, but ultimately, as God gauges it, we will be successful. Wisdom will give us discernment, perception, insight, intuition, and especially the ability to sense danger ahead of time.

Wisdom thinks ahead, before the fact. "If the serpent bites before being charmed, there is no profit for the charmer." In a more relevant setting, wisdom says, "Don't think about seeking counsel after you're in the ditch. Seek counsel *before* you fall."

And how do we get this wisdom? According to James 1:5 we must pray for it: "But if any of you lacks wisdom, let him ask of God, who gives to all men generously and without reproach, and it will be given to him."

> "Wisdom has the advantage of giving success. If the serpent bites before being charmed, there is no profit for the charmer" (Eccl. 10:10b-11).

> "My son, if you will receive my sayings, and treasure my commandments within you, make your ear attentive to wisdom, incline your heart to understanding; for if you cry for discernment, lift your voice for understanding; if you seek her as silver, and search for her as for hidden treasures, then you will discern the fear of the Lord, and discover the knowledge of God" (Prov. 2:1-5).

> "For the Lord gives wisdom; from His mouth come knowledge and understanding. He stores up sound wisdom for the upright; He is a shield to those who walk in integrity, guarding the paths of justice, and He preserves the way of His godly ones. Then you will discern righteousness and justice and equity and every good course" (Prov. 2:6-9).

God promises to give wisdom to us in abundance. It is essential, however, that we *ask* God for it.

But praying is just one part of the process in gaining wisdom. Let's balance this promise from the New Testament with a few verses from the Old Testament. Getting wisdom is the result of mutual effort. It's a matter of working together with God in pulling off a wise lifestyle. God doesn't deliver wisdom at our door like the morning paper. Wisdom doesn't come in a neat package, like a carton of cool milk that's sitting there waiting to be opened. It's the result of a cooperative effort. To verify this, read Proverbs 2:1-5 very carefully.

Each "if" represents another condition—our part in the process. And the "then" statement gives the result of meeting those conditions. "Then you will discern the fear of the Lord, and discover the knowledge of God."

The result of receiving and treasuring God's Word, of making our ears attentive and including our hearts is discovering the knowledge of God. It is discerning what it means to fear the Lord. Wisdom provides such perspective.

We've been digging. We've been listening. We've been sensitive to His Book. We've been learning from His truths. We haven't been sidelined by all the seductions of our times. We haven't even been driven by our emotions! We hear that God has spoken in His Word and we're attentive to what He has said and we won't let Him go until He gives us insight into how to put it into practice and handle a given situation. That's smart. It's straight talk from God, with a promise to boot!

Summarize the thoughts stated in Proverbs 2:1-9 to record God's promise to you.

God says, "_____ (your name)

IF you will _____

_____

THEN I will _____

_____.

If we walk in integrity, we will not stumble. What a great thought! If we decide that we will live honestly, we will not stumble into dishonesty.

Week of **FEBRUARY 20**

We will model honesty. God promises He will honor that. He will protect us. Ultimately we win over the ungodly. He stores up sound wisdom for us. He gives us a shield of protection as we walk in integrity.

Wisdom doesn't come easily. It may start with prayer, but there's so much more. God will do His part if we'll do ours. We all want to hit the mark, to live the rest of our lives on target. But we know we cannot do it apart from the wisdom of God.

Read Jude 24-25. Respond to God's promise to keep you from stumbling by writing a prayer of commitment and thanksgiving below:

_____

_____

_____

day Five

A Fool's Portrait

THE EXTERNAL ACTIONS OF A FOOL

A close look at Ecclesiastes 10:12-20 reveals at least four ways a fool demonstrates his or her folly.

Mouth and Words (10:12)
Who is it that suffers the most in the life of a fool? The fool himself. He may make others miserable, but he's the one who is "consumed." He utters words that lead to his own suffering and sometimes demise.

Have you ever tried to work with and give counsel to a fool? Don't waste your time. Rather than hearing counsel, the fool dominates the conversation. He starts talking on the wrong basis, so you can imagine what the end of his talk will be. You would think the person would stop and realize how far off base he or she really is. The fool just multiplies words.

"Words from the mouth of a wise man are gracious, while the lips of a fool consume him" (Eccl. 10:12).

> "No man knows what will happen, and who can tell him what will come after him?" (Eccl. 10:14).

Future and Predictability (10:14)

According to James 4:13-16, what did James call a person who arrogantly predicts future plans? (circle)

Foolish   Well-prepared   Evil   A leader

What attitude does a wise person have toward future plans? _____

If you have teenagers in your home, I'll bet you've used some similar lines: "If you keep acting like that, there's no telling where you're gonna wind up." Or, "How many times do you have to learn the same lesson? If you keep doing that, such and such might very well happen. I mean, who knows where you'll be in two years, to say nothing of the end of your life?"

> "The toil of a fool so wearies him that he does not even know how to go to a city" (Eccl. 10:15).

Confusion and Stupidity (10:15)

The fool exhausts himself by his inefficient and unproductive lifestyle. He gets so confused, he doesn't even know how to go to a city. If Solomon were writing today, perhaps he would put it this way: "The person is out to lunch." It doesn't mean they're intellectually defective. Fools can be very bright. I've met fools with impressive graduate degrees. I have seen fools with extremely high IQs. Folly has nothing to do with IQ. But it has everything to do with stupidity! His talk is empty prattle.

> "Through indolence the rafters sag, and through slackness the house leaks. Men prepare a meal for enjoyment, and wine makes life merry, and money is the answer to everything" (Eccl. 10:18-19).

Procrastination and Poor Judgment (10:18-19)

There are sagging rafters and a leaky roof. The house has been neglected because of procrastination. Even the courtroom of the king lacks fine appointments and disciplined servants because the king's life is an endless routine of food, amusement, booze, and stupid comments about money. There's wasted time; there's a loss of priorities; there's a careless lifestyle; there's a lack of discipline toward unfinished tasks. Even though there are so many things to take care of, irresponsibility and verbosity abound.

DEALING WITH A FOOL

Our thinking will break down if we stay in the presence of and try to do verbal battle with a fool. If we try to outsmart a fool, outtrick a fool, outfight a fool, or outtalk a fool, we will lose!

Week of FEBRUARY 20

Read Proverbs 14:7. What command does the Bible give on dealing with a fool? _____

What will happen if you choose not to obey that command? _____

Our tendency as Christians is to extend encouragement and affirmation forever, which is commendable. And so we come up with statements like, "We ought to use kind and thoughtful words so they'll understand."

Honorable treatment *is* appropriate—for as long as one can remain sane and safe. But there's a limit! There comes a time when honor doesn't fit a fool. Those are not my words. I'm quoting from the Scriptures (see Prov. 26:1,8). We no longer take all of the sharp edges off so that life becomes comfortable for the fool—we allow the sharp edges to stay.

God doesn't rush to their rescue and say, "Oh, I know it must hurt to suffer the consequences of a fool. Let me relieve you." God says, in effect, "You forfeit the right to those blessings if you live against Me."

Now, in that condition, they break. They repent. They turn. Look at Psalm 107:17-18. They waited until conditions became extremely serious. *Then* they cried. They cried out to the Lord in their trouble, and He saved them in their distress. He called in the support of affection and affirmation and encouragement. But *not until* they came to the end of themselves. There are times, my friend, when love must be tough. But when there is brokenness and true repentance, restoration is appropriate. When there is restoration from folly, the redeemed then proclaim the story!

> "Like snow in summer and like rain in harvest, so honor is not fitting for a fool" (Prov. 26:1).

> "Like one who binds a stone in a sling, so is he who gives honor to a fool" (Prov. 26:8).

> "Fools, because of their rebellious way, and because of their iniquities, were afflicted. Their soul abhorred all kinds of food; and they drew near to the gates of death" (Ps. 107:17-18).

Based on the portrait of a fool from Ecclesiastes 10:12-19, would you say you are dealing with a fool at this point in your life? ❑ Yes ❑ No ❑ Not sure

Depending on who the foolish person is, what action is God's Word commanding you to take?

❑ Leave the presence of the fool.
❑ The foolish person is in my family. I can't leave, but I can withhold honor to give God room to work.
❑ That fool is me and I need to get right with God.

NOTES

To the Leader:

Read Ecclesiastes 10:1. Prayerfully evaluate your role as a teacher. Is there an area of foolishness that is destroying your effectiveness as a teacher? Are you talking too much? Preparing too little? Does your lifestyle back up your words? Do you seek recognition or lasting results? Pray for undefiled wisdom so you can influence others to choose wisdom.

leader Guide

Before the Session

1. Obtain a chess set or other strategy game and a dartboard.
2. Write each letter of SUCCESS vertically down the left side of a poster board.
3. Enlist volunteers to be prepared to read Psalm 46:10; Proverbs 12:16; 15:1-2,18; and 19:11.

During the Session

1. Display the chess set and ask: *In games involving strategy are you ruthless, clueless, or cautious? Which approach brings success? Why? Does that same approach guarantee success in life? Why?* Discuss the first question in Day 1. OR Display the SUCCESS poster and encourage participants to create an acrostic, using words that begin with each letter to describe success. Record responses on the poster. (Responses may include smart, unbeaten, conquer, competitive, excel, strength.)

2. Read Ecclesiastes 9:10 and remind participants that last week's lesson ended with Solomon's encouragement to work hard at everything you do. However he then admonished his readers not to depend on their own abilities as they seek success. Invite a volunteer to read Ecclesiastes 9:11. Lead the class to compare Solomon's attitude toward success with the world's definition. Request participants state a common saying about the only two things certain in life (death and taxes). Ask what Solomon would say are the two certainties of life (time and chance). Request someone read Ecclesiastes 9:12 and ask what can happen to successful persons who are as slippery as fish or quick as a bird. Inquire: *Since evil can happen so quickly and unexpectedly should we live in fear all the time? What point is Solomon making?*

3. Request a volunteer read Ecclesiastes 9:13-18. Lead participants to explore the "above the sun" wisdom (signified by the italicized statements) discussed in Day 2. Encourage them to give present-day illustrations of those statements. Ask: *What makes life so loud? Why doesn't God shout or force us to listen? What must we do when life*

Week of **FEBRUARY 20**

is loud? Encourage learners to use Elijah's example from 1 Kings 19:11-13 to answer that question. Invite the volunteer to read Psalm 46:10. Lead a discussion on what it means to be still and how that helps believers hear God and gain wisdom.

4. Request someone read Solomon's parable once again in Ecclesiastes 9:13-15. Ask: *Did that poor wise man achieve success? Why?* Point out success isn't always achieved in recognition but in the ultimate result. In Ecclesiastes 10 Solomon brings out the truth that even when wisdom doesn't get the recognition it deserves, it is still better than foolishness. Invite someone to read Ecclesiastes 10:1-3. Help participants explore the advantages wisdom brings to a person's private life. Ask participants to give examples (without naming names) of how a little bit of foolishness can overshadow wisdom in a person's life.

5. Read Ecclesiastes 10:4-7. Ask participants to state principles from this passage that will help them display wisdom at work. Acknowledge the person at the top may lack wisdom and enjoy manipulating and humiliating others. Request participants listen for advice on how to handle that kind of boss as volunteers read Proverbs 12:16; 15:1-2,18; and 19:11. Call for specific ways those proverbs can be put into practice. Request participants complete the final activity of Day 3 as you read Ecclesiastes 10:8-10 aloud. Lead a discussion on how these verses challenge adults to display wisdom in their social relationships.

6. Ask why participants agree or disagree that wisdom is knowing when you lack wisdom. Read aloud Ecclesiastes 10:11 and Proverbs 16:18 and lead the class to discern the principle stated in both verses. (Don't be too proud to seek counsel.) Ask what two ways Dr. Swindoll said we can gain wisdom. Lead learners to explore Proverbs 2:1-9 to discover how they can work "together with God in pulling off a wise lifestyle."

7. Ask participants to name four ways a fool demonstrates folly (Day 5). Ask how a wise person deals with a fool. Request someone read Proverbs 14:7. Ask: *Why don't we always obey that command? What if the foolish person is someone you can't leave—what do you do then?*

8. Display a dartboard or draw a target on the board. Ask what defines success for an archer. Inquire: *How does an archer achieve success consistently? How can we consistently attain and display wisdom to keep our lives on target?*

9. Close in prayer by reading aloud Jude 24-25.

NOTES

Charles SWINDOLL

What Are You Waiting For?

day One

God's Uncommon Counsel

> "Cast your bread on the surface of the waters, for you will find it after many days. Divide your portion to seven, or even to eight, for you do not know what misfortune may occur on the earth. If the clouds are full, they pour out rain upon the earth; and whether a tree falls toward the south or toward the north, wherever the tree falls, there it lies. He who watches the wind will not sow and he who looks at the clouds will not reap. Just as you do not know the path of the wind and how bones are formed in the womb of the pregnant woman, so you do not know the activity of God who makes all things. Sow your seed in the morning and do not be idle in the evening, for you do not know whether morning or evening sowing will succeed, or whether both of them alike will be good" (Eccl. 11:1-6).

The last two major sections of Solomon's journal could be summed up in three commands: Be bold! Be joyful! Be godly! Solomon's personal remarks, as he nears the end of his journey, are full of refreshing hope.

God gives our generation four commands in 11:1-6, each in strong contrast to advice we hear today. Read those verses in the margin.

Instead of protecting, release yourself! This first piece of advice is implied in Solomon's opening comment: "Give generously." And the command has a promise: "you will find it after many days." When a life is released to others, there is something remarkable about God's faithfulness in bringing back benefits and blessings.

Read Luke 6:38 in your Bible. State the principle of this verse with an "If ... then ..." statement.

_____

Releasing ourselves is God's way. He honors unguarded vulnerability. But how exactly do we do that?

Rather than hoarding, give and invest. "Divide your portion." Let the benchmark of your life be bold, unselfish, broad-based generosity. It isn't just giving to our families or giving to the person who is personally attracted to us or to whom we are attracted. It's giving broadly.

In place of drifting, pursue! Before we deal with this piece of advice, let's track where Solomon's coming from (11:3-4). He is probably describing people who spend their lives observing the obvious and noting the inevitable. Instead of occupying ourselves with the obvious, we should

Week of FEBRUARY 27

pursue life! There are things we cannot change. We cannot change the weather, taxes, bills, people's responses, time, or death. We can worry about them all we like, but we can't change them!

Cast your bread on the waters. Divide your portion and *don't keep track*. Don't wait for letters of thanks. Don't expect to get rich or have your name in lights. Don't expect to be reciprocated—just go for it! Pursue this thing called life!

As an alternative to doubting, trust! This encourages us to courageously trust the living God. As you sowed in the morning, press on in the evening. Don't hang a "Do Not Disturb" sign on the door knob of your life.

The only way we can come to terms with reality is by trusting God, *regardless*. We can't wait for conditions to be perfect.

What have you been waiting for to fully trust God?

- ❏ A fuller understanding of God's ways
- ❏ A healthy savings account
- ❏ My kids to grow up
- ❏ To grow up myself

YOUR MISSION, SHOULD YOU CHOOSE TO ACCEPT IT

Allow me to wrap up today's study with several direct words of challenge. The first has to do with getting started.

Start activating your life today and never quit. Find someone to invest in. Give yourself to a local church. Locate a school to which you can give time and energy. Volunteer for service. Refuse to let your life collect dust. Don't wait for the weather to change. Don't wait for the kids to grow up. Don't wait for conditions to be perfect. Start today and never quit.

What's your passion—what do you love to do?

_____

How can you use that passion in service to others? List everything you can think of.

_____

_____

"Just as you do not know the path of the wind and how bones are formed in the womb of the pregnant woman, so you do not know the activity of God who makes all things. Sow your seed in the morning and do not be idle in the evening, for you do not know whether morning or evening sowing will succeed, or whether both of them alike will be good" (Eccl. 11:5-6).

Based on the passage above, what are three things you can't possibly understand?

1. _____
2. _____
3. _____

What should you do when life is not understandable?

_____

_____

Remember that wisdom must accompany action. When we read about "living life to its fullest" we tend to become supermotivated. We want to put on roller skates and dash out into life half cocked. That's not God's counsel. Start today, but start with wisdom. Ask God how you can invest a slice of your wealth in something other than that which will return to you.

Watch out for enemy attacks during a lull in the action. There will be periods of time that aren't very exciting. There will be times of low tide and little production. We all have them, and they're hard to endure. But during those lulls in the action, be careful of enemy attacks. The enemy will say things like: "It's not worth it. Give it up. Don't waste your time." Even though a few people will try to point out all the dangers, press on.

day Two

Enjoy Life Now, Not Later

"Indeed, if a man should live many years, let him rejoice in them all, and let him remember the days of darkness, for they will be many. Everything that is to come will be futility. Rejoice, young man, during your childhood, and let your heart be pleasant during the days of young manhood. And follow the impulses of your heart and the desires of your eyes. Yet know that God will bring you to judgment for all these things. So, remove grief and anger from your heart and put away pain from your body, because childhood and the prime of life are fleeting" (Eccl. 11:8-10).

We are given permission to enjoy life. Solomon says: "The light is pleasant, and it is good for the eyes to see the sun" (Eccl. 11:7).

Throughout Scripture, references to light and sunshine are used to describe the warmth of God's love. When we focus on Him, He lifts the gloom and takes the stinging pain of depression out of life.

Read Ecclesiastes 11:8-10 in the margin. When do you have the best chance for happiness? (check one)
❑ **When I'm young and looking ahead to life.**
❑ **When I'm middle-aged, established, and financially secure.**
❑ **When I'm retired and get senior discounts at restaurants.**
❑ **Happiness is possible at any age.**

We don't have to wait until we reach some magical age when we are allowed to crack open the door and slip silently into the realm of happiness. It's there for us to enjoy *throughout* our days.

The second thing about enjoying life is that *all the traditional limitations are removed.* Many would say to be happy you must be young.

Week of FEBRUARY 27

That's a traditional thought. But if I read this correctly, it is saying that if you should live many years, there is happiness to be claimed right now!

The third thing Solomon says about enjoying life is: *God inserts just enough warnings to keep us obedient.*

Underline those warnings in Ecclesiastes 11:8-10.

"If a man should live many years, let him rejoice in them all, and let him remember [however] the days of darkness [or he'll be disillusioned], for they shall be many" (11:8). As we instruct our children on how to live, let's be sure they have a lot of fun when it's the years for having fun. But let's do our very best to guard them from disillusionment.

"Don't let those great days throw you. There are a lot of things that will come to be futility." The emphasis should be placed on *things.* "Son (daughter), if you begin to be preoccupied with the *things* in life and you allow yourself to focus mainly on *things*, those *things* will ultimately leave you empty. They will demand of you more than they give you."

In verse 9 Solomon warns youth, "Relax and enjoy your childhood and your adolescent years. Yet, don't forget—there'll be a day of accountability." Some may think the warning takes all the joy out. But I see a great deal of God's compassion. He's concerned that we not go wild with our liberty. What insane lives we would live if there were no anchor on the tether, if we forgot there is a God to whom we will someday answer!

I see a God of compassion leaning out of heaven and saying to His people, "So [I plead with you], remove vexation from your heart" (11:10). We don't use the word *vexation* often. The original Hebrew term is a combination of two ideas—anger and resentment. And when you place anger alongside resentment, then blend them together, you get rebellion.

Rebellion has no age limit. This mixture of anger and resentment is what Solomon has in mind when he refers to vexation. And God says, "In your pursuit of happiness, you need to put aside a rebellious spirit."

Some people need professional help in knowing how to put aside the rebellious spirit. Rebellion is often so ingrained that they are unable on their own to remove the roots that made them that way—the way they were raised, the habits they have cultivated, and even their mentality.

While we are told to "Go for it!" we are also warned to "put away pain from your body." I doubt Solomon is writing in symbolic language.

How can parents present Solomon's encouragements and warnings in Ecclesiastes 11:8-10 to a:

Preschooler

_____

Elementary-age child

_____

Teenager

_____

College student

_____

Newlywed

_____

Middle-aged adult

_____

Why not take this comment literally? It makes a lot of sense if we understand it to mean: "Get rid of the things that bring the body pain." Take a straight look at what alcohol does to your body. Take an honest look at what drugs do to your body. Look at the effects of tobacco. Face it straight on and realize the pain your body will be forced to endure if you participate in those harmful activities. Those things can bring pain to your body. Your liberty must include some limitations!

Solomon tells us why: "Because childhood and the prime of life are fleeting." You have only one childhood, only one adolescence. What you do with your life now is the memory you'll have through all your tomorrows.

What pain do you need to put away from your heart and body? Circle all that apply
Anger   Harmful substances   Unhealthy foods
Immorality   Other: _____

A Long-Awaited Insight

At long last, Solomon says it (12:1)! I've wanted to tell him to "remember the Creator in the days of his youth" since chapter 1. But now he sees it on his own. And he openly admits it's best if a person makes such a discovery on his own.

"Remember your Creator when you are young" means to act decisively on behalf of the living God. This means we realize *He is the one essential ingredient we need for a truly happy lifestyle.* It means we will not follow the dictates of our own heart, but the dictates of His truth. It means we will make an intelligent, serious, independent study of what Scripture says about how to walk in obedience. We will remember our Creator.

"Remember also your Creator in the days of your youth, before the evil days come and the years draw near when you will say, 'I have no delight in them' " (Eccl. 12:1).

day Three

What Hinders the Pursuit of Happiness?

I can think of only two things that could hinder one's pursuit of happiness. *Self-appointed excuses keep us from claiming daily joy.* There are dozens of excuses that keep us from enjoying each day God gives us.

Week of FEBRUARY 27

The second thing is *a self-styled independence that keeps us from remembering our Creator*. Does this sound familiar? "I'll make it on my own, thank you. I've made it this far on my own. I know where I'm going and I'm going to get there." The sound of independence.

Read Psalm 118:24 in your Bible. What days should bring happiness to our lives? (circle)

Wedding day　　　**Christmas day**
Every day　　　　**Graduation day**

What must we remember if we are to find cause for rejoicing every day? _____

Happiness is not that complicated. If my relationship with the living Lord is in place, if I take His perspective and look at my life as it unfolds in the valleys as well as on the mountain, happiness accompanies me.

But when I take on life (including God) with a grim determination that says, "I'm going to get what I want," I sometimes get it, but happiness is never a by-product. In fact, those are some of the darkest days of my life. Happiness eludes me—just as it does everyone else. The only way we can enjoy life is to find God's gift of happiness in Jesus Christ.

At long last Solomon has come to realize the importance of listening to and walking with his Creator. The sneering cynicism we found earlier in his journal is now conspicuous by its absence.

"Remember Him ... *before* the evil days come." Let that sink in. Solomon calls them "evil" days. Any investment in evil pays a dreadful dividend—consequences, scars, bad habits. It affects us mentally and emotionally. It slows down our maturing process and dulls us spiritually. "No," says Solomon emphatically. "I tried that route and it's an empty journey!"

Read Psalm 25:6-7 in your Bible.

What can you ask God to remember? _____

_____

What can you ask God to not remember? _____

_____

"Remember also your Creator in the days of your youth, before the evil days come and the years draw near when you will say, 'I have no delight in them'; before the sun, the light, the moon, and the stars are darkened, and clouds return after the rain; in the day that the watchmen of the house tremble, and mighty men stoop, the grinding ones stand idle because they are few, and those who look through windows grow dim; and the doors on the street are shut as the sound of the grinding mill is low, and one will arise at the sound of the bird, and all the daughters of song will sing softly. Furthermore, men are afraid of a high place and of terrors on the road; the almond tree blossoms, the grasshopper drags himself along, and the caperberry is ineffective. For man goes to his eternal home while mourners go about in the street. Remember Him before the silver cord is broken and the golden bowl is crushed, the pitcher by the well is shattered and the wheel at the cistern is crushed" (Eccl. 12:1-6).

A Fresh Look at Physical Aging

I don't know of a more eloquent allegory in all the Old Testament regarding aging than Ecclesiastes 12:1-6.

Record phrases from 12:1-6 that tell what happens to our bodies as we age.

_____

_____

By the time we reach the end of Solomon's list, we realize the value of his great counsel to remember our Creator. Let's not wait until we are white-haired to respond!

Solomon's words eventually impact all of us. The wonderful thing about the Bible is that its predictions and warnings are not only absolutely reliable, they are timeless. There will come a day when we'll have to face the inescapable factors of mental slowness and physical infirmity. It is the way God planned it. So come to terms with reality *now*.

If the journal stopped right here, it would leave us with a very grim picture. If all we could look forward to in life were gray hairs and fewer teeth, then I'd call that a bleak future. But there is much more. There *is* something to smile about! What is it? "Remembering the Creator." That puts a smile on the face of the aging. When His perspective is inserted, it is like a ray of light hitting a prism and suddenly beautiful colors shine through. It's fabulous! It's amazing what He does with guilt and self-pity and feelings of uselessness and fear. His prism of color and beauty just dances all around life. And death? All it does is open a new door.

Read Psalm 63:4-8. When did the psalmist remember God? _____

What actions did the psalmist take to remember God?

_____

What was the result of the psalmist's remembrance of his Creator?

_____

Week of FEBRUARY 27

day Four

Life's Final Factor

"Then the dust will return to the earth as it was, and the spirit will return to God who gave it" (12:7). You won't read about this in *Time* or *Newsweek* or see this presented on the television news tonight, but take it from God, it will happen. You may live a bit longer, then you will die. After death, what? "The spirit *will* return to God who gave it." If you are ready, you will see a smile like you've never seen in your earthly life. It will be on the face of your Savior. You'll hear Him say, "Come into My kingdom." You'll hear sounds you never heard on earth. It's beautiful! Not even the aging process will cancel out His plan to make you a new person, fitted for eternity.

> **Read 1 John 3:2 in your Bible. What will your new person be like when you are changed?** _____
> **Why?** _____

But what if you don't accept this relationship with the Lord? "Vanity of vanities … all is vanity!" At the end of life, all you'll have to claim is a feeling of futility. Life is a challenge. Life is tough. And only the power of Jesus Christ can give you the resiliency to handle it. I cannot imagine how anyone copes apart from a relationship with Jesus Christ.

> **If your life ended today, what would meet you? (circle)**
> God's welcoming smile   Futility
> **How is God calling you to pray in response to what you just circled?** _____

PRACTICAL ADVICE BETWEEN THE LINES

Three very practical and useful statements are woven between the lines of Solomon's comments. First: *I must face the fact that I'm not getting any younger.* Aging is a reality of life. People who try to dodge or deny the fact that they are getting older are kidding themselves.

Second: *God has designed me to be empty without Him.* God has designed you and me to experience a vacuum without Him. He planned us to be restless without Him. All the way through this journal we have been reminded that God has made life boring on purpose. Why? So that we would discover that beauty and color and songs of joy come only from following His directives, not from human counsel.

Third: *Now is the time to prepare for eternity.*

Read 2 Corinthians 6:1-2 in your Bible. How can you prepare for eternity today? _____

_____

Have you prepared for life beyond retirement? If you have, you can smile at whatever life throws at you. You have the hope of looking into the Savior's face and hearing Him say, "Welcome home!"

You and I do not have a thing to fear simply because we are growing older. If our faith is firmly fixed in the Savior, we can count on Him to be waiting up for us. Our room is all ready. The light is on. We are expected. He will welcome us home.

day Five

A Closing Confession

> "In addition to being a wise man, the Preacher also taught the people knowledge; and he pondered, searched out and arranged many proverbs. The Preacher sought to find delightful words and to write words of truth correctly" (Eccl. 12:9-10).

If we expect to find happiness in life, we must get *above* the sun. And that is precisely what Solomon does as he turns the final page of his journal. Unless we connect with the living God through faith in Jesus Christ, life is reduced to an empty existence.

Solomon now moves into a brief autobiographical section which is quite personal. In this unusual section, the Preacher analyzes his craft. It is a rare body of information of special interest to anyone whose responsibilities include the communication of God's truth (12:9-10).

Solomon's opening remark should never be forgotten: the preacher, first and foremost, is to be a wise man. His primary task is to teach the

Week of FEBRUARY 27

people knowledge. In doing so he is to do certain things—"ponder," "search out," and "arrange." When he mentions "ponder," he uses the term that means he weighs the words carefully. He sifts through their implications. He feels them. He compares them. He debates himself over them. He wrestles and sweats over them.

As dogs worry over a bone, so it is with a good preacher. He works on words. His craft is words. He searches diligently. He tries to find just the right words, which requires careful search. And such research is often exhausting.

In Solomon's search for truth, he attempted to find just the right words. And did he ever! "A time to be born, and a time to die. A time to mourn, and a time to dance." Who will ever forget those words?

If you hear good sermons from your minister week after week, it isn't because he's creatively shooting from the hip. It is because he's doing his homework. Hard work is taking place in his study: searching, digging, meditating, reading, arranging thoughts, thinking it through, getting at it, refusing to surrender to sloth. In a word, diligence.

Why go to all that trouble? Solomon says the reason is that the preacher is seeking to find delightful words. The term *delightful* means "winsome, easy to grasp, readily applied."

Solomon's style and word pictures penetrate the fog of preoccupation. They awaken us to the significance of his message.

If you have enjoyed these Bible studies from Dr. Swindoll and desire to purchase your own copy of his book Living on the Ragged Edge, look for the coming re-issue of this volume from W Publishing Group in February 2005.

**Read Ecclesiastes 12:11 in the margin.
What words of wisdom from Ecclesiastes have painfully pricked you like a nail? _____**

_____

How has the truth that those words came from your Shepherd helped you endure the pain? _____

_____

"The words of wise men are like goads, and masters of these collections are like well-driven nails; they are given by one Shepherd" (Eccl. 12:11).

Words are like tent spikes, riveting thoughts into the mind. When there is nobody around and we turn off the light and let our head sink into the pillow, there are words that haunt us. They keep us awake. "The Word of God is alive and active, sharper than a two-edged sword" (Heb. 4:12).

165

> "Beyond this, my son, be warned: the writing of many books is endless, and excessive devotion to books is wearying to the body" (Eccl. 12:12).
>
> "The conclusion, when all has been heard, is: fear God and keep His commandments, because this applies to every person" (Eccl. 12:13).
>
> "Because God will bring every act to judgment, everything which is hidden, whether it is good or evil" (Eccl. 12:14).

What truths from "the ragged edge" have:

challenged you?

_____

encouraged you?

_____

What changes have you made in your life as a result of this study?

_____

_____

Solomon closes with words addressed to his son. He has held off counseling his son until now. And what he says will make every student in school today sigh with agreement. Even faculty members have been known to say "Amen" after reading verse 12. It's not only true on a school campus, it's equally true in life.

THE CONCLUSION

Read Ecclesiastes 12:13. What did Solomon conclude about life after all of his exploration and experimentation? Underline your answer.

I love the anti-climactic ending to this incredible journal. We've been with Solomon through every conceivable emotion, but now he finishes the entire work by saying that there are two things we need to pay attention to—two "musts." First, we must *take God seriously*. Hold Him in highest regard. Respect and revere Him. Second, we must *do what He says*. Obey Him. You'd think Solomon slammed his journal shut and said, "Got it done. Got it said." But that's not all.

He knew his readers would ask why. Why should I revere God? Why should I obey His truth? Verse 14 explains his reason. In the final analysis, we'll do business with God. Count on it. The One who made us has every right to hold us accountable. All alone, standing face-to-face with God in that epochal moment, we will give an account of the life we have lived.

Do you want to know how to handle your life in light of such a day of reckoning? Would you like to know the secret? The password? Christ. He alone is the way, the truth, the life. Without "the way," there is no going. Without "the truth," there is no knowing. Without "the life," there is no living.

Remember Him now. If you are young with most of your life stretching out before you, remember Him, believe in Him. Act decisively on His behalf. Even if you're not young, remember Him. Jesus Christ is the only One who has the ability to wash away your sins and give you a new perspective. This conclusion to Solomon's journal can be your introduction to joy and forgiveness, hope and peace.

Come to terms with reality, my friend. Only through Him can you and I ever hope to endure life's ragged edge.

Week of FEBRUARY 27

leader Guide

Before the Session
1. Make a list of common axioms. You can find many by conducting an internet search using the keyword *clichés*.
2. Prepare a worksheet for each participant with these instructions: Read the following Scriptures and answer the questions. Deuteronomy 5:15; 8:2,18; Nehemiah 4:14; Psalm 42:5-6; 77:11; Luke 22:19; 2 Timothy 2:8. 1) What are we to remember about God? 2) Why should we remember God?
3. Conduct a personal commentary study of Ecclesiastes 12:1-8.

During the Session
1. Ask: *What is the best/worst advice you've ever been given?* Solomon offered three commands in the conclusion to his journal—Be bold! Be joyful! Be godly! Have you ever been given this advice—if so, how was it worded? How might your life have been different if you had received and followed those three commands? OR Organize the class into small groups. Give each group several moments to come up with as many clichés or advice-giving sayings as possible. (You may need to share some sayings from the list you compiled to get their creative juices flowing.) Allow groups to share. Guide the class to find similarities between the sayings on their lists and Solomon's advice in Ecclesiastes 11:1-6. (For example, "Don't put all your eggs in one basket" could reflect the advice in 11:2.)
2. Request a volunteer read the first italicized statement of advice from Day 1. Guide participants to reword this statement so it reflects the world's advice. (For example, "Protect yourself at all costs.") Ask whether Solomon's advice or the world's advice makes the most sense and why. Invite volunteers to share their response to the first activity in Day 1. Call for the second italicized statement of advice and again ask the class to reword it to reflect the world's values. Invite the class to follow along in their Bibles as you read aloud Luke 12: 16-21. Ask: *Did the rich man follow God's wisdom or the world's wisdom?*

NOTES

To the Leader:

Read the material related to Ecclesiastes 12:9-10 in Day 5 again and substitute the word "teacher" for "preacher." How will you allow these words of wisdom to transform your teaching?

NOTES

What did it gain him? What did God call him? How would you describe a person who is rich toward God?

3. Call for volunteers to read the third and fourth italicized statements in Day 1. Again lead the class to reword them from the world's viewpoint. Request a volunteer read Ecclesiastes 11:3-4. Help learners understand Solomon was saying we'll never get anything done if we wait for perfect conditions. Discuss the second activity of Day 1. Read aloud Philippians 3:12-14 and guide participants to explore how the apostle Paul reflected Solomon's advice to trust God and press on despite imperfection.

4. Ask someone to read Ecclesiastes 11:7-10. Use the material in Day 2 to review Solomon's encouragements and warnings about enjoying life. Ask: *Does verse 9 offer good, bad, or risky advice? Why? Is this similar or opposite from what you were taught? How is this balanced advice?* Guide the class to complete the activity in the margin of Day 2.

5. Discuss the first activity of Day 3. Ask: *Is happiness a condition or a choice? How does this verse compare to Solomon's encouragement in Ecclesiastes 8:15?* Ask a volunteer to read Ecclesiastes 12:1. Distribute the worksheet you prepared earlier and complete the activity together as a large group (or organize the class into small groups and assign one or two passages to each group to explore).

6. Read Ecclesiastes 12:1-8 and explain the allegories. Ask how believers can remain joyful despite the reality of aging and death. Discuss the first activity of Day 4. Ask: *When did your parents quit viewing you as their child? How did this make you feel? When does God quit viewing you as His child? How does this make you feel? When is it too late to heed Solomon's advice in this latter part of his journal?*

7. Discuss the first activity of Day 5. Read aloud Hebrews 4:12-16. Ask how this passage describes the pain God's Word can bring and the grace available through the Shepherd. Invite a volunteer to read Ecclesiastes 12:13. Ask participants if they agree or disagree this is an anticlimactic ending to Solomon's journal and why. Ask what Solomon's conclusion tells us about the complicated lives we often lead. Encourage participants to explore how that conclusion helps persons rejoice all the days they're given on earth. Allow volunteers to share their responses to the activity in the margin on page 166.